ANGEL'S EYES

CHRISTMAS ANGELS

GERRY CULLEN

ISBN-13: 9798862002904
ISBN-10: 1477123456

Cover design by: Art Painter
Library of Congress Control Number: 2018675309
Printed in the United States of America

THIS BOOK IS DEDICATED TO

MY MUM AND DAD

WONDERFUL COUNSELLOR ... I AM HIS MESSENGER

- ARCHANGEL GABRIEL

CONTENTS

WHITE FEATHERS APPEAR

WHEN ANGELS ARE NEAR

Angel's Eyes and it's follow up Chrismas Angels is my third book to be published.

It was inspired out of the "gift" I received, after being in a coma, at Leeds General Infirmary, in March 2018.

Angel's Eyes was written originally as a 12 part drama for television in September 2018. I quickly followed it up with a 4 part Christmas Angels drama. Both series are set in LEEDS and the ancient city of YORK.

I realised I needed more stories to complete my adaptation from TV series into book format.

This book is a modern day series of stories featuring ordinary people in extraordinary situations.

I had never written books or for Television prior to having open heart surgery.

My very real and true story continues today.

WHAT TV PRODUCTION
COMPANIES ARE SAYING

ABOUT

ANGEL'S EYES/CHRISTMAS ANGELS

I have just finished reading your script for Angel's Eyes.
It's fascinating hearing your story about how you have developed a love for writing since your coma. I hope you are in good health now!

I think it's fantastic that you are writing so much, so many other writers can only dream of the productivity you have, so definitely keep it up!

I think you have an exciting opening to the episode with Rebecca saving the woman at the train station in Leeds, potentially revealing her identity to the public.

I think the whole premise of the show is also really interesting. There's also a lot of potential for humour there with these slightly out of touch angels returning to earth.

I think there are funny lines throughout! I loved the crying Mary statue being caused by the rusty pipe and then the Monsignor asking if it had been an act of God!

I also really liked your sections with the angels not understanding modern day things like Marvin Gaye and people calling each other love.

One thing I would recommend is increasing the amount of conflict in your episode concerning the ghostly Roman Centurian problem at the museum in York.

Don't make it too easy for John Paul to solve the problem with the Centurian. We need that to be incredibly difficult to solve so that it creates lots of conflict and drama for John Paul. More tension adds to the story line!

I think you have a nice climax to the episode in which the angels are forced to jeopardise their identity to save a woman with the press close by.

All in all I found Angel's Eyes to be thoroughly entertaining with memorable characters and wonderful atmospheric settings in Leeds and York.

- LIVERPOOL PRODUCTION COMPANY

As a footnote, the conflict with the Roman Centurian and the cohort of Roman soliders has now manifested into several stories throughout the book.

The ghostly Centurian is truly an obstinate individual who thinks he is still on a mission. The Angels have their work cut out when dealing with him, as you will see, in the coming stories.

ANGEL'S EYES

The Angel private eyes with a difference undertake anything with a twist … they are all real angels!

Angel's: Rebecca, Mary, John-Paul, and Nicola have been sent by Michael the Archangel to LEEDS, West Yorkshire, and the ancient city of YORK to investigate all types of problems from all levels of society.

The Angel's are aiming to find, and guide, lost souls, to protect and help those who are in distress, to help those without a cause.

They have been charged to give sight to those who cannot see, whatever the problem, and to heal the sick and incurable.

All the angel's will have to undertake their assignments while also being human on Earth at the same time!

They do not want to get their wings … they already have them!

While under the protection of Heaven they will be able to cloak themselves in disguise!

The Angel's are ready to help whoever needs their help in this stylish series of stories!

The Angel's will encounter the Gray Lady, the ghostly Centurian and a cohort of Roman soldiers, Dick Turpin, and Guy Fawkes along the way. They will also experience Speed Dating and various problems in a modern World.

CHRISTMAS ANGELS

This seasonal set of stories reunites Rebecca, Mary, John Paul, and Nicola.

They have been reassigned by Michael the Archangel and assume the roles of Proprietors of the famous CHRISTMAS ANGELS shop in YORK, on a short-term lease … with a view to being permanent!

However, they are shop keepers with a difference!

They become engaged in various angelic and human situations … all with a magical Christmas feeling!

The stories take place at various settings in YORK.

Will the Angels be found out or will their true identities remain an angelic secret?

CHRISTMAS ANGELS

ANGEL'S EYES IT'S WRITTEN IN THE STARS

When Michael the Archangel dispatches Angels ... Rebecca, Mary, Nicola and John Paul to Leeds and York they are given special powers to deal with certain human tasks while maintaining their secret identities!

Michael's spiritual advice. Arrival Park Square, Leeds, and the Bar Convent in York. Having total protection. A challenging situation ...

In the realms of Heaven ...

"The eyes are the windows to the soul ... and the soul allows the eyes to see everything, everywhere" advises Michael the Archangel

"You have all been selected to go on a mission ... God's mission" advises Michael

"You will take human form on Earth, yet still retain your Heavenly powers and no one will come between you and God. For God is God ... the one and only who has sent you" advises Michael

"He is known only by the name "I am" advises Michael

"If anyone asks who has sent you ... tell them "I am" has sent you" says Michael

"You are not on a mercy mission!" advises Michael

"Whatever you bind on Earth shall remain so and no one will be able to change it!" advises Michael

"You are above everything, yet you will be human and angelic at the same time!" says Michael

"Keep your identities secret ... only I and God will know who you really are!"

"You have all been specially selected" informs Michael

"What if we are found out?" asks Rebecca

Rebecca is angelic, striking and has long brown hair and blue piercing eyes ...

"You will all look after each other." advises Michael

"Angel's Mary, Nicola and John-Paul will also be with you Rebecca ... you will not be alone!" says Michael

Mary is angelic, striking, has long blonde hair and blue eyes. Nicola has long wavy brunette hair and attractive. John-Paul is tall, dark, and good looking.

"You will receive the Holy Spirit ... for nothing is above or below your powers ... but you must use them wisely by also using discretion." advises Michael

"Cloak yourself in The Truth and what is real!" advises Michael

"No one will suspect you and you will have the benefit and wisdom to change your appearance at the wink of any eye" says Michael

"You are being sent to heal broken lives and guide those who are lost whether already dead or left behind to bring them all back into God's Kingdom!" advises Michael

"... but what if they won't listen?" asks Mary

"Whatever you bind on Earth Mary will be considered bound in Heaven ... for those sins you retain ... you retain!" advises Michael

"Where are we being sent Michael?" asks John-Paul

"There seems to be a need in Yorkshire, England!"

"Yorkshire ... where's Yorkshire?" asks John-Paul

"All in good time John-Paul" advises Michael

"Can you tell us anything?" asks Nicola

"We are sending you to a place called Leeds and the ancient city of York!" advises Michael

"In York you will reside at the Bar Convent close to the city centre" says Michael

"You'll all have large cities under your wing" says Michael

"Similarly, a place has also been prepared for you in Leeds" advises Michael

"How do you know all these things?" asks Mary

"You shouldn't ask that question!" advises John Paul

"We know all things in Heaven, Mary" says Michael

"You may encounter ghostly apparitions in York" advises Michael

"Why, what happened there?" asks Nicola

"Not too long ago, a sighting happened while excavation work was being carried out!" advises Michael

"What did they see?" asks Rebecca

"Ghosts coming towards them" says Michael

"A ghostly legion of Roman Soldiers marching and going through walls chanting" advises Michael

"Do not worry ... if you encounter such beings ... you will all be protected ... let the worries of today be enough" advises Michael

"Tell us about our assignments in Leeds and York" asks Nicola

"Yes ... what about Leeds?" asks Mary

"Leeds is a large city in West Yorkshire ... it is the beating heart of the county, and it has two major hospitals ... so you will have work to do" says Michael

"Why?" asks Nicola

"You'll find out … your files are ready at the offices prepared for you!" advises Michael

"When do we start, Michael?" asks Rebecca

"Immediately!" advises Michael

"Immediately?" asks Mary

"A place has been prepared for all of you in Leeds. Remember, you will all be of human form, your wings will be disguised and unable to be seen by human eyes, you will appear ordinary!" advises Michael

"However!" advises Michael

Michael continues …

"You may encounter spiritual humans who can contact the dead … all of this is before you" says Michael

"Lost souls are needing your guidance … they are awaiting your arrival." advises Michael

"Then we all must leave at once" advises John-Paul

"I agree … your mission is before you" says Michael

Then, as if in an instant, all the Angels suddenly arrive at Park Square in Leeds!

"A very smooth arrival" says John Paul

"I didn't feel a thing" advises Mary

"Rebecca are you alright?" asks Nicola

"I think so" replies Rebecca

"What about you Nicola?" asks Mary

"Yes, I'm OK … strange clothes we have to wear" responds Mary

"Very strange indeed" says John Paul

"Remember, we're all mortal here on Earth!" advises Rebecca

"We're not really … are we?" asks Nicola

"No, of course not!" advises John Paul

"Where are we?" asks Mary

"Leeds … don't you remember what Michael said?" advises John Paul

"I remember" says Mary

"Well, this looks like the place" advises Rebecca

"How do you know Rebecca?" asks Mary

"Look at that" says Rebecca

"What is it?" asks Mary

"That is a sign" advises John Paul

"A sign that reads … ANGEL'S EYES INVESTIGATIONS" advises Rebecca

"It has a meaning" advises John-Paul

"What does it mean?" asks Mary

"ANGELIC NETWORK for GUARDIAN ENFORCEMENT of LAW SPECIALISTS –

"ANGEL'S" replies John Paul

"That's us" says Mary

"It's all a bit of a mouthful" says Nicola

"Yes, but utterly true … I like it" advises Rebecca

"What's amazing is that all of this has been set up by Michael" says John Paul

"We're all truly speechless" says Mary

"We have been given a wonderful start and we will all do our absolute best to help anyone who wants our assistance" says John Paul

They all enter the second-floor premises in Park Square … suddenly another voice greets them …

"May I help you?" asks the voice

"Hello … we're the new owners!" advises Rebecca

"Hello … My name is Kate … I am your Private Secretary and associate to the business … Welcome … I have been expecting you!" responds Kate

Kate is in her mid 20's, petite with long dark hair and green eyes …

"Thank you, Kate, … I am Rebecca, this is Mary, Nicola and well that is John Paul"

"I know all about you!" advises Kate

"Not everything, I hope!" replies John Paul

"I have been advised that … well, your different in your approach to helping people" says Kate

"Really … we are different in lots of ways … and one day we will be able to tell you … but until that day …" advises John Paul

"Maybe you're the answer to our prayers?" asks Kate

"Maybe" advises Nicola

"Have you come far?" asks Kate

"Somewhere … far away from here … you could say we have been reassigned" advises Rebecca

"Reassigned?" asks Kate

"Yes … to help anyone who wants our help" advises Nicola

"You're all as trendy as the sign" says Kate

"Trendy?" asks Rebecca

"It's not a word we're familiar with" says John Paul

"Oh, it means … kind of up … you know with it" says Kate

Oh trendy, now I get it" says Rebecca

"With it … I like it … well I suppose we are" says Nicola

"What about John Paul?" asks Mary

"What about me?" responds John Paul

"Well Kate … what do you think?" asks Mary

"He's very well put together … quite the man about town" says Kate

"Man about town … now that's original!" says John-Paul

"I like that" laughs John Paul

"Don't let it go to your head" says Rebecca

"Don't worry I won't!" replies John Paul

"Touchy" says Kate

"Now … first port of call … follow me, I will show you the office suite … and the work waiting for you" advises Kate

"Is there a lot to do?" asks Nicola

"Probably … remember that's why we're here!" says John Paul

The office suite is on the second floor. It is tastefully decorated and has a certain amount of ambience …

"This way" advises Kate

"We have lots of clients already on our books!" says Kate

"We share the building with Solicitors and Barristers, so help is at hand!" advises Kate

"… just in case we need them" says Kate

"Just in case?" asks Mary

"Thanks Kate lead the way … we are all ready to go and meet the clients that need our help" says John Paul

Kate leads Rebecca, Mary, Nicola, and John Paul into another room …

"This is our reception, where I and Angelica work" advises Kate

"This is Angelica" says Kate

Angelica is a tall, slim young blonde with a beaming smile …

"Angelica … this is John Paul" advises Kate

"Hi Angelica … lovely to meet you … what a wonderful name" says John Paul

"Hello … lovely to meet you too" beams Angelica

"Where are my manners … this is Rebecca, Mary, and Nicola my associates, you could say we specialise in helping people" advises John Paul

"Do you help lost souls?" asks Angelica

"How did you know?" asks Nicola

"We help those lost from all walks of life" advises Rebecca

"Well, I am here to help you, like Kate … if there is anything you need let me know" replies Angelica

"Then there's Peter" says Kate

"Peter?" asks Rebecca

"Oh, he's a troubled and misguided young man" says Kate

"Maybe you could start with Peter?" asks Angelica

"Maybe, maybe" responds Mary

"Have you travelled far?" asks Angelica

"Further than you think" says Rebecca

"… but it was an omen that we should come here to help you" advises Mary

"You'll find our investigations uplifting and rewarding … truly dazzling" advises John Paul

"Dazzling?" asks Kate

"Oh, were different from the others" says Mary

"That's enough for now" advises John Paul

"We'll settle in … read the files and advise you where we're going" advises Rebecca

The phone starts to ring …

"Excuse me while I get that!" says Angelica

Mary and Nicola are taken by surprise …

"Don't be alarmed … that's a modern invention called the telephone" says John Paul

Angelica looks serious …

"Yes … I will send someone over straight away … don't worry" says Angelica

The call ends …

"Who was that … Angelica?" asks Kate

"A call from someone at the Cathedral" replies Angelica

"It sounded serious" says Rebecca

"Yes, I'm afraid it is" advises Angelica

"Give me all the details … we'll get on to it straight away!" says Rebecca

"Well … it's quite different … something we're not used to" advises Angelica

"The Cathedral advise that a woman has suddenly been taken ill" says Angelica

"Wouldn't it be better if they called for an ambulance?" asks Kate

"I'm sorry Kate" says Angelica

"Sorry for what?" asks Kate

"… it's your Mum" advises Angelica

"My Mum … my God" replies Kate

"What's God got to do with it?" asks Nicola

"Everything" says Rebecca

"OK … don't worry Kate … I will go with Rebecca" says John Paul

"I'm coming with you!" replies Kate

"OK … Mary and Nicola will accompany you" says John Paul

St Anne's Roman Catholic Cathedral in Leeds was built between

1901 and1904.

There has been a Cathedral on the site since 1878. It is the centre of the Catholic diocese of Leeds. It is very ornate, and the building is used by worshipers and parishioner's from everywhere.

Rebecca, John Paul, Mary, and Nicola take the short journey out of the second-floor office suite on foot and proceed with Kate down the Headrow …

They walk in front of the emphatic Town Hall which is a 19th century municipal building in the heart of Leeds.

St Anne's Roman Catholic Cathedral is just a short walk ahead …

"OK this way" advises Kate

"Don't worry Kate … your Mum will be alright" says Nicola

"How do you know?" asks Kate

"Just believe what Nicola has told you" advises John Paul

"All you have to do is believe" says Nicola

They all arrive at the entrance of St. Anne's Cathedral …

An early morning mass has been stopped by the priest and parishioners are astonished … one of them is administering first aid …

"Is she alright" asks Kate

"Kate … your Mum was asking for you" advises the priest

"I'm here Mum … hold on" says Kate

"What's your Mum's name Kate?" asks Nicola

"Bernadette" advises Kate

"What happened?" asks Rebecca

"We think she suffered a seizure" advises the priest

"The ambulance and responder are on their way from Leeds General Infirmary" advises a parishioner

"What do you think John Paul?" asks Rebecca

"We need to act fast ..." responds John Paul

"What do you mean?" asks the priest

"This lady is dying ... now let us do our job" says Rebecca

"Who are you?" asks the priest

"It is all right Father ... they are with me ... we are all business associates ... we work together" advises Kate

"Yes ... but what do they know about saving your Mum's life?" asks the priest

"We'll take care of it, Father" says Nicola

"How?" asks the priest

"We have advanced methods of medication ... where we come from, we regularly administer this type of procedure" says Rebecca

"Come from ... come from where?" asks the priest

"Please Father ... let them do their job" insists Kate

The Priest nods at Kate's request ...

"Please all leave the church" asks John Paul

"Why?" asks the priest

"We need to give this lady room and a fighting chance of living" says Rebecca

"OK ... please leave the church" asks the priest

Several parishioner's leave by the side door as requested ...

"You too Father" asks Rebecca

"Please do as they say" says Kate

"What about me?" asks Kate

"Mary will look after you" advises Nicola

Kate also leaves with the Priest and Mary ...

The Cathedral is now empty ...

John-Paul, Rebecca and Nicola lay their hands on Kate's Mum ...

"Bernadette you are amongst friends ... you will feel a glow" says John Paul

Bernadette's body begins to radiate ... within mines she sits up ...

"Are you alright Bernadette?" asks Rebecca

"Where am I?" asks Bernadette

"You're in Saint Anne's Cathedral in Leeds ... don't you remember?" says John Paul

"Yes, I remember" says Bernadette

"What happened?" asks Bernadette

"You fell asleep" says Nicola

"Fell asleep ... I don't understand" says Bernadette

Kate and Mary return with the Priest ...

"Is Bernadette alright?" asks the priest

The ambulance and responder arrive on the scene ...

"Where's the patient?" asks the responder

"Here" advises the priest

"... but she looks fine" says the responder

The Priest and ambulance crew are all astonished ...

"Bernadette ... are you alright?" asks the priest

"Who healed you?" asks the responder

"Kate ... where's Kate?" asks Bernadette

There is no sign of Kate. She has left the scene with JohnPaul, Rebecca, Mary, and Nicola ...

Bernadette does not remember anything ...

Back at the 2nd floor suite in Park Square ... no one is the wiser for what

happened at the Cathedral. Kate has no recollection whatsoever of anything ...

"OK Rebecca … I will bring in the files to you" says Kate

"Thank you, Kate" says Rebecca

"Do you think she suspects?" asks Mary

"Highly unlikely" says John Paul

"Both she and her Mum had a narrow escape today" says Rebecca

"No one suspected us at the Cathedral" advises John Paul

"Looks like we're going to have lots to do in Leeds" says Rebecca

"Just as Michael said … it is going to be vastly different, and we are working with lost souls" advises John Paul

"The Angels agency is our cover … no one will suspect us" says John Paul

"Remember we were once human too … we will work wonders here" advises Rebecca

Back at the Cathedral a pile of white feathers has been found after the healing of Bernadette took place …

"Where on Earth did these come from?" asks the priest

"I don't think Earth has anything to do with it" responds the Monsignor

"Remember the saying … when white feathers appear … angels are near" says the priest

"Really?" says the Monsignor

"I wonder" advises the Monsignor

IN A MATTER OF MOMENTS

The Angel's encounter Leeds General Infirmary and Jimmy's (St James Hospital). Mary remembers the 1920's while their curiosity gets the better of them. They visit the Jubilee Wing in the LGI and find a patient in need. There is no response. The laying of hands. Will Bernard be cured? Keep our secret. A promise made and broken …

XXIX

"*The sunrise was beautiful today*" says Rebecca

"*Maybe we need to explore the city for our next case?*" asks Mary

"*Maybe not!*" says Rebecca

Kate enters the office suite …

"*Good morning, Rebecca*" says Kate

"*Good morning, Mary*" smiles Kate

"*Hi Kate … how are you?*" asks Rebecca

"*Oh, fine … fine*" responds Kate

Sirens start to wail outside …

"*Whatever is that noise?*" asks Mary

"*Oh, you will hear plenty of that. It is either an ambulance heading for the LGI or Jimmy's or the Police!*" advises Kate

"*The LGI … Jimmy's?*" asks Mary

"*What does that mean?*" asks Rebecca

"*Everyone knows it as Jimmy's*" says Kate

"*The LGI is reference to Leeds General Infirmary and Jimmy's refers to St James Hospital just outside the city*" advises Kate

"*Jimmy's … why is it called Jimmy's?*" asks Mary

"*Oh, it's affectionately known as that by the people of Leeds*" says Kate

"*St James … how did he get on to it?*" asks Mary

"*A question that one day will be answered Mary*" advises Rebecca

"*Tell me … is the LGI far?*" asks Rebecca

"*Oh no it's not far from here … you can reach it on foot*" says Kate

"*I must see what happens in this place*" says Rebecca

"*Oh, you remember Rebecca … remember the 1920's?*" says Mary

"*The 1920's?*" asks Kate

"Mary is referring to a period we studied in history" says Rebecca

"Times have changed" says Kate

"Indeed, they have" says Rebecca

"We must visit this hospital and see for ourselves" says Mary

"I agree Rebecca" says Kate

"It's all a bit sci-fi now" advises Kate

"Sci-fi?" asks Mary

"You know … advanced" advises Kate

"In what way Kate?" asks Rebecca

"In medicine … saying advanced is only a reference" advises Kate

"Now I understand" says Mary

"Advanced" asks Rebecca

"But we're …" says Mary

"That's quite enough Mary" advises Rebecca

"Your what?" asks Kate

"What Mary is trying to say is that we were not aware of the advancement in medicines" advises Rebecca

The door opens and in walks another character … Peter

"Good morning, all" says Peter

"I take it your Peter" asks Rebecca

"Yes … the one and only" replies Peter

Peter is in his early thirties, has blue eyes and dark haired …

Kate steps into the conversation …

"Peter this is Rebecca and Mary … the new owners of ANGEL'S EYES INVESTIGATIONS" advises Kate

"I see you've wasted no time in changing the company name" says Peter

"We thought it would be more in line with our investigations"

advises Rebecca

"We are both intrigued with the General Infirmary here in the city centre" saysMary

"Oh, the LGI" responds Peter

"We would like to go there" advises Rebecca

"I'll take you there if you want me to?" says Peter

"Naturally ... I think that would be a great idea" says Rebecca

"When?" asks Peter

"Well, there's no time like the present ... what about now?" asks Mary

"I agree" says Rebecca

"OK, let's go now" says Peter

"Both I and Mary will accompany you" says Rebecca

"We may be some time Kate" advises Peter

"That is fine ... don't worry I will start putting the caseloads together for Nicola and JohnPaul ... they should be here later" advises Kate

"Nicola and JohnPaul?" asks Peter

"They are both our associates and will be working from our office in York" advises Rebecca

"I didn't know there was going to be an office in York" says Peter

"Well, our Boss at Head office has arranged it all" says Rebecca

"Your Boss ... I guess he must be important?" asks Peter

"You could say that" advises Rebecca

"He is the top man next to ..." says Mary

"Next to whom?" asks Peter

"The main man of course" replies Rebecca

"Now lead the way to the Infirmary Peter" asks Rebecca

"Yes ... we may be needed there" says Mary

"Why?" asks Peter

"Why will you be needed there?" asks Peter

"You ask a lot of questions Peter" says Rebecca

"Are you wanting or looking for answers?" asks Mary

"Answers to what?" says Peter

"Everything?" says Rebecca

"Can't you see without asking questions?" says Mary

"You should remember this … seek not to know all the answers but to understand the questions" advises Rebecca

"Now I perfectly understand Rebecca" says Mary

"To be really honest with you, we are wanting to satisfy our curiosity that's all" advises Rebecca

"Curiosity?" asks Mary

Rebecca takes Mary to one side …

"Careful Mary you very nearly gave the game away twice … in a matter of moments" says Rebecca

"Remember what Michael said … use discretion" advises Rebecca

"Sorry Rebecca … I will remember that in future" says Mary

Rebecca and Mary decide to go to the LGI …

"OK Peter … lead the way" asks Rebecca

All three arrive on foot at The Jubilee Wing of Leeds General Infirmary and it is not too long before Angels, Rebecca and Mary, are firmly thrust into action …

An emergency ambulance arrives on the scene … blue lights flashing …

It is a cardiac arrest …

"We've tried everything" advises a paramedic to the A&E Doctor

"Any response?" asks the Doctor

"Very little response ... and we need to act fast" advises the paramedic

"Let's get him into A&E immediately" says the paramedic

"Check his pulse rate and rhythm nurse" asks the Doctor

Mary whispers to Rebecca ...

"We may have to act fast Rebecca" advises Mary

"Remember what Michael said ... nothing is above or below our powers and we can cloak our disguise in the wink of an eye" advises Rebecca

In a flash Rebecca and Mary take on another disguise assuming the roles of nurses in A&E ...

"Can we help Doctor?" asks Rebecca

"Where did you spring from?" asks the doctor

"Cardiac" responds Rebecca

"We are specially trained in Cardiac cases" advises Mary

"Where did you say you were from?" asks the Doctor

"Oh, we're from Cardiac ... we're here to help you" insists Rebecca

"OK if you can help here ... watch over the patient" advises the Doctor

"I'll get my kit" says the doctor

Mary tries to help the patient ...

"What's your name" asks Mary

"Bernard ... can you help me?" asks the patient

"We'll try" advises Rebecca

Both lay their hands on Bernard and a miraculous bright light appears.

"What's going on?" asks Bernard

Time stands still. The glow of the light lasts several minutes. Bernard is now cured and in recovery ...

"What have you done?" asks Bernard

"We have cured you … tell no one … your pain and cardiac arrest has gone" advises Rebecca

"Who … what … how?" asks Bernard

"We are angels" advises Mary

"Angels?" asks Bernard

"Yes, sent by God" replies Rebecca

"He heard your pleas … your life has been saved" advises Rebecca

"Where are you going?" asks Bernard

"Our work is done here … we are on our way to help others … tell no one what has happened" says Rebecca

"How can I thank you?" asks Bernard

"By keeping our secret!" responds Mary

"Secret?" asks Bernard

"Thank you" says Rebecca

Rebecca and Mary instantly change back into their human form, and they are no longer Cardiac nurses … and leave A&E …

The Doctor returns … "What's happened?"

"Where are the nurses from Cardiac?" asks the doctor

"I'm cured" says Bernard

"Cured?" asks the Doctor

"Cured by whom?" says the Doctor

"A miracle … Angels … beautiful Angels … they took away all my pain and cured me" insists Bernard

"Angels?" asks the Doctor

"Don't you mean the two nurses from Cardiac?" says the Doctor

"It's a miracle I tell you … a real miracle" says Bernard

The more Bernard is questioned the more he tells his story!

"We told him to tell no one Mary" advises Rebecca

"Yes, but he didn't keep his promise" says Mary

"No matter … God works in mysterious ways His wonders to perform" advises Rebecca

"Will Michael be proud of us Rebecca?" asks Mary

"I think he would be more than proud Mary" responds Rebecca

Reporters from the Evening Post newspaper arrive on the scene …

"I'm Jack Davies … can I get a statement?" asks the Reporter

"The patient has just been through quite an ordeal" advises the doctor

"Maybe if you could tell us what happened Doctor?" asks Jack

The Doctor relays his version of the story to the reporters and they are quite astonished at what they are hearing …

"Was anything left at the scene?" asks Jack

"In what respect?" asks the Doctor

"Evidence" asks Jack

"Evidence of what?" asks the Doctor

"They were more than Cardiac nurses … they were angels? advises the reporter

News of the angel's curing Bernard is all over the LGI by now but who are these wonderful creatures and who sent them?

Were they Messengers from God?

"There will be many more who need our help" says Mary

"Remember why Michael sent us here" advises Rebecca

"Yes, Rebecca I do" insists Mary

"However, we must be aware that others may seek us out … to expose us" says Rebecca

"They must never be allowed to succeed" advises Rebecca

"What will Nicola and John-Paul have to say about our first mission?" asks Mary

"It is more than likely they will relish the fact that we have helped someone in need and saved a life ... there are many, many more who need saving ... this is only just the beginning" advises Rebecca

Arriving back at Park Square, Rebecca and Mary tell Nicola and John-Paul about their brush with humanity and how they saved the day at the LGI.

"It was very satisfying and rewarding" advises Rebecca

"Yes, indeed it was" replies Mary

"Did you manage to retain your cover?" asks John Paul

"Undoubtedly ... everything remains intact" advises Mary

"You have created quite a stir at the LGI you know" advises Nicola

"In what way?" asks Rebecca

"It appears that the Cardiac nurses who saved Bernard were not of this World" says Nicola

"Well, we did use our cover to our best advantage" says Rebecca

"Didn't we Mary?" asks Rebecca

"Oh, yes to our full advantage John Paul" says Mary

"Why ... did we do something wrong?" asks Rebecca

"No ... quite the opposite you followed Michael's instructions completely" says John Paul

"It was all for the greater good John Paul ... for the greater good" advises Mary

"I agree ... that gentlemen you saved ... he is talking of a miracle" says Nicola

"Bless Bernard" says Rebecca

"Maybe it was ... maybe the miracle was him saving us" says Mary

"Saving you?" asks Nicola

"Remember, we were all once human too in the past" says Rebecca

"It's the future that worries me" says John Paul

"Don't worry John-Paul ... we know our place and that God is with us" advises Mary

"Now let us look at the case files ... ask Kate to bring them in as soon as possible" asks Rebecca

Meanwhile, back at A&E in the LGI, Jack stumbles on some evidence near to where Bernard had been cured ... two white feathers ...

"Remember the old saying Sarah?" asks Jack

"What's that Jack?" replies Sarah

"When white feathers appear ... angels are near" advises Jack

"I thought it was just a saying Jack?" responds Sarah

"No ... it's more than just a saying" advises Jack

"In what way?" asks Sarah

"Believers really do believe that angels are near ... and in this case they tie into the patient being cured" advises Jack

"So, a miracle really could have taken place here?" asks Sarah

"Yes, I think it does imply that" advises Jack

"What next?" asks Sarah

"Well, we will take the feathers for analysis and see what comes back from the lab" advises Jack

"As in a DNA test?" asks Sarah

"Yes, we could be on to something here" advises Jack

"And if we find nothing?" asks Sarah

"We find nothing" says Jack

"It will serve as a reality check ... the DNA is our only hope" advises Jack

"Hope?" asks Sarah

"There may be a pattern immerging one way or another" advises *Jack*

ANGEL'S OF THE NORTH

John Paul and Nicola are in conversation at the Bar Convent in York. Making peace with God. A beam of heavenly light. Excavations in York. Can you help my friend?

Early morning, 2nd floor suite, Park Square, Leeds … ANGEL'S EYES INVESTIGATIONS AGENCY …

"Well, I've read all the casefiles" advises Rebecca

"Have you decided which case to choose?" asks Mary

"Yes" responds Rebecca

"Well, what have we decided to investigate next?" asks Mary

"I think we should start with a lady called Marie" advises Rebecca

"Is she a special case?" asks Mary

"She seems to need our spiritual help that's for sure" advises Rebecca

"In what way?" asks Mary

"I think it's a matter of seeing before we can do anything Kate" advises Rebecca

"Does she live nearby?" asks Mary

"The address is across the city" advises Kate

"We must see Marie today ... we will phone first of course" advises Rebecca

"Phone?" asks Mary

"Remember we are of human form on Earth, and we have to appear so Mary!" advises Rebecca

"How?" asks Mary

"We must conform and fall in line with human contact ... we will phone this morning" advises Rebecca

Rebecca picks up the receiver and begins to dial Marie's number ...

The phone starts to ring ...

"Hello this is Marie ... how can I help you?" says the voice

"Oh, hello my name is Rebecca ... of the Angel's Eyes Agency?"

"Oh, yes I remember" says Marie

"We believe you're in need of our help?" asks Rebecca

"That's right ... in more ways than one" replies Marie

"How can we help you?" asks Rebecca

Rebecca is on the line for a few minutes and makes a note of what Marie has told her ...

"We've read your file ... we specialise in helping people" advises

Rebecca

"Can we call to see you this morning?" asks Rebecca

"Yes, that would be helpful ... do you have satellite in your car? asks Marie

"Satellite?" asks Rebecca

"Yes, if you enter my address and postcode, it'll bring you right to the door" says Marie

Rebecca shrugs ... "We have our own way of finding you ... we will be with you shortly" advises Rebecca

Meanwhile, John Paul and Nicola are taking up residence at the Bar Convent in York ...

The Bar Convent is a living heritage centre. It is also known as the Convent of the Blessed Virgin at Micklegate Bar, York. It is the oldest surviving convent in England, and it was established in 1686.

The laws of England, at that time, prohibited the foundation of Catholic Convents and because of this, the convent was both established and operated in secret.

John Paul pulls the doorbell ...

A few minutes later someone answers the door...

"Good morning ... I am Joseph ... welcome to the Bar Convent" says the voice

"Thank you for such a warm welcome" greets John Paul

"We understand a reservation has already been made for us?" asks Nicola

"Under what name?" asks Joseph

"Michael" advises Nicola

Joseph checks the log and finds both Nicola and John Paul on his roster ...

"Ah yes, the agency" answers Joseph

"We have been specifically given instructions by Michael that you

both should have the best in hospitality and a suite of offices have been made available as requested" advises Joseph

"Michael is always known for being thorough" advises John Paul

"I will give you the guided tour and show you your living quarters which are located next to your office suite" replies Joseph

"Thank you" says Nicola

"Do you plan to stay in York long?" asks Joseph

"Long enough to complete our assignments" advises Nicola

"Assignments?" asks Joseph

"We are looking into various matters on behalf of the Church ... you know hush hush!" advises John Paul

"I quite understand" advises Joseph

"York is very atmospheric ... you'll soon find yourselves at home here" says Joseph

"It's steeped in history" advises Joseph

"Are you from this area?" asks Joseph

"Oh, we're from across time" says Nicola

"Across time?" asks Joseph

"What Nicola means is that we're from afar" says John Paul

"Let's just say we've travelled many miles to be with you" advises Nicola

"York is a wonderful ancient city ... we need to take in all it has to offer before we take up our new roles" advises John Paul

"That would be a clever idea ... I will be your guide" says Joseph

"We really shouldn't take up too much of your time, Joseph" advises Nicola

"It really is no bother ... I would love to show you round" insists Joseph

"OK we agree" advises JohnPaul

"*Your hired as our official York tour guide*" *says Nicola*

"*When would you like to go into the city?*" *asks Joseph*

"*Well, there's no time like the present ..." says John Paul*

"*I agree ... what about you Nicola?*" *asks Joseph*

"*So do I*" *says Nicola*

"*Then the first place we should start is where everyone starts really, at the Minster ...*" *advises Joseph*

"*We'll take the tour on foot ... it's the easiest way of getting around York*" *advises Joseph*

JohnPaul and Nicola follow closely behind Joseph ...

"*This is Deansgate ... and as you can see behind is the magnificent York Minster ... built in the Seventh Century, it is one of the largest of its kind in Northern Europe. The Minster is the seat of the Archbishop of York*" *advises Joseph*

"*It's very impressive*" *says John Paul*

"*An amazing piece of architecture*" *says Nicola*

"*Why have all the statues been removed from its frontage?*" *asks John Paul*

"*Oh, that was King Henry the Eighth's orders*" *advises Joseph*

"*Orders to remove statues?*" *responds Nicola*

"*Anything to do with Catholicism was removed*" *advises Joseph*

"*And what replaced it?*" *asks Nicola*

"*Oh, the Church of England, run exclusively by Henry*" *informs Joseph*

"*He had a massive fall out with Thomas Moore*" *advises Joseph*

"*Catholics were basically hunted down*" *advises Joseph*

"*Guy Fawkes was another born in the city ... now he tried to bring down the Houses of Parliament with the gun powder plot*" *advises Joseph*

"Houses of Parliament?" asks John Paul

"Oh, Westminster in London ... the seat of government" advises Joseph

"Then ... there's the King" advises Joseph

"Who Henry?" asks Nicola

"No ... King Charles who has just taken over from the Queen" informs Joseph

"Taken over?" asks John Paul

"Sadly, the Queen died recently" advises Joseph

"Now we're all Charles's loyal subjects ... but it's a modern monarchy now" advises Joseph

"I must get to know more about King Charles" says Nicola

"You will ... all in good time" advises Joseph

"Patience Nicola ... let Joseph continue our fascinating tour" responds John Paul

Meanwhile, back in Leeds, Rebecca and Mary arrive at Marie's house in the Roundhay Park area ...

It is situated 3 miles north of the city. The Park covers more than 700 acres, and it is one of the biggest in Europe.

Marie's 3 bedroomed semi-detached house is close by ...

"Well, this is it Mary" advises Rebecca

"I'll ring the bell" says Rebecca

A well-rounded woman in her early 50's answers the door ...

"Marie?" asks Rebecca

"Ah, you must be from the agency?" replies Marie

"Yes, we are" replies Rebecca

"I'm Rebecca ... this is Mary my associate" advises Rebecca

"Sorry for the cloak and dagger ... we have to be very careful today" *says Marie*

"Very wise" replies Mary

"Come in ... this way" advises Marie

Marie leads them into the lounge ...

"Welcome to my home ... can I offer you some refreshments?" asks Marie

"A cup of tea would be nice" replies Mary

"Coming up ... I have just made a brew" advises Marie

"Please be seated ... we don't stand on ceremony here!" laughs Marie

"Ceremony?" asks Mary

"That was a joke" replies Marie

"We've read your case file Marie ... how can we help you?" asks Rebecca

"Maybe you can?" says Marie

"What seems to be the problem?" asks Mary

"Can you help me with regards to life's torments?" asks Marie

"Torments?" asks Mary

"Ask of us what you will Marie" replies Rebecca

"Tell us your story ... and we'll see how we can help you" advises Mary

"Well, it goes like this ... you see everyone has left me" advises Marie

"Left you?" asks Mary

"I'm all alone in life" replies Marie

"Have you thought about getting a pet ... a cat or a dog?" asks Mary

Rebecca intervenes ... "I don't think that's what Marie is talking about" says Rebecca

"Go on Marie ... tell us more" asks Rebecca

"Well, I am an only child ... I have never married but I have stayed

true to my upbringing and faith … I am a Catholic" advises Marie

"Good start" says Mary

"Sush Mary … let Marie tell us her story" advises Rebecca

"Can you help me to make peace with God before I go?" asks Marie

"Where are you going?" asks Mary

"My time is almost near … but I'm afraid" advises Marie

"How do you know your time is near?" asks Rebecca

"I've been told that I have terminal cancer" advises Marie

"We're sorry to hear that Marie" replies Mary

"Don't be afraid" advises Rebecca

"God loves us all … and there is nothing to be afraid of" says Mary

"How do you know?" asks Marie

"We are angels … real angels and we're on God's mission" replies Rebecca

"Yes, it's true" advises Mary

"Rebecca, haven't we forgotten something?" asks Mary

"We haven't disguised our identities" advises Mary

"It's alright Mary … if Marie truly believes she'll keep our secret" replies Rebecca

"Yes … I genuinely believe" advises Marie

"What are you going to do?" asks Marie

"We intend to lay our hands on you" advises Rebecca

"Will it help?" asks Marie

"Yes, your doubts and fears will all fade away … there will be no more loneliness. God is with you always" advises Rebecca

A beam of light radiates from the Angels …

Mary and Rebecca place their hands on Marie …

The beam of light suddenly fades …

Mary sits up advising she feels vastly different to how she was before …

"Thank you … all praise to God … I can see clearly now, and I am no longer afraid" advises Marie

"I'm ready to enter God's Kingdom" says Marie

"Thank you for all you have done for me … is there anything I can do for you?" asks Marie

"Don't tell anyone what happened here … keep our secret … there are so many more souls that need to be saved" advises Rebecca

"I promise to keep your secret safe" says Marie

Back in York, John Paul, Nicola, and Joseph decide to visit a coffee shop in the Shambles … more questions follow …

"Why are there so many excavations being done in the city?" asks Nicola

"Oh, York is a maze of history, at every turn and every corner" advises Joseph

"Take for instance this coffee shop in the Shambles" says Joseph

"Why is this place called the Shambles?" asks John Paul

"It is a very historic street and as you can see there are many preserved medieval buildings, some of them date as far back as the

14th century!" informs Joseph

"Go on, this is fascinating" advises Nicola

"The street is narrow, and it has many timber framed buildings with jetted flooring … it is one of York's most famous landmarks" advises Joseph

"Why is it so crowded?" asks John Paul

"York is always crowded with tourists … they come here from all over the world" advises Joseph

"Such is the attraction of the ancient city of York" says Joseph

John Paul, Nicola, and Joseph start to walk down the Shambles towards the Rose of York …

What is this place?" asks Nicola

"Is it a hotel?" asks John Paul

"Hardly … it's a public house" replies Joseph

"Public house … does everyone live there?" asks John Paul

"No … it's a place of relaxation, somewhere you can have a beer" advises Joseph

"A beer … what's that?" asks Nicola

"Let's go inside and I'll show you" advises Joseph

No sooner have Joseph, John Paul and Nicola entered the Rose of York when an unfortunate incident begins to take place …

A young lady in distress calls out …

"Please can someone help me … my friend is having a fit?" says the voice

"What do they mean … having a fit?" asks Nicola

"She's having a seizure … and they need medical help" advises Joseph

"Maybe I can help?" asks John Paul

"I'd be glad Sir, if you could … my name is Trish" advises the young woman

The Bar manager comes over to see if he can help …

"Can I help you?" asks the Landlord

"Please can you call for an ambulance?" asks Joseph

The Bar manager disappears and makes the emergency call …

He dials 999 to report that a young woman needs urgent medical attention …

"Emergency … which service do you require" asks the operator

"Ambulance" advises the Landlord

"Location?" asks the operator

"The Rose of York pub in the Shambles" advises the Landlord

"We know it … paramedics and an ambulance are on their way" replies the operator

The Landlord notifies Joseph then disappears back into the crowded bar area.

"Paramedics and an ambulance are on their way" advises the Landlord

"Thanks" says Nicola

"Let me place my hand on her" says John Paul

"Please make her comfortable" says Nicola

A glowing light begins to radiate from the now unconscious woman …

Almost immediately the young woman responds and sits up …

"What happened?" asks Diane

"Don't you remember Diane … you had a fit?" advises Trish

"Sorry I don't remember anything" advises Diane

"You just suddenly blacked out" says Trish

"There was nothing I could do" says Diane

"You had a seizure … and you could have died had it not been for this kind gentlemen who intervened" advises Trish

"Where is he … I must thank him?" replies Diane

When everyone looks around, John Paul, Nicola and Joseph are no longer on the premises …

"Where is he?" asks Diane

"Who was he?" asks Diane

The Landlord advises …

"No one knows … he was a stranger to our city" says the Landlord

"An angel" says Diane

"He saved my life" insists Diane

"He was a real angel" says Diane

The Paramedics and ambulance are now on the scene at the Rose of York ...

"What happened?" asks a paramedic

One of the paramedics looks to the floor and finds two white feathers ...

"What is this?" asks the paramedic

"Two white feathers" answers the Doctor

"See I told you, he was an angel" insists Diane

"Come on ... you need to be assessed in A&E" advises the paramedic

The Landlord clears the bar area and Diane and Trish are taken out to the responder which speeds its way through to the city hospital.

A TRULY KIND OF WONDERFUL

Feeling human love. The Press investigating. Saving a Life. Situation averted.

Vision of the future. Encountering problems at Lendal Bridge. Don't throw your life away. Is God's kingdom far? The promise.

PARK SQUARE, LEEDS CITY CENTRE, 2ND FLOOR, IN THE HALLWAY NEAR TO THE ANGEL'S OFFICE SUITE …

"Hi … I am Steven O'Hare, one of the solicitors … you could say we are neighbours" *says a voice*

"Call me Steve" *advises the voice*

Steve is tall, dark, and handsome and fits the bill oozing charm …

"Hello, I am Rebecca … this is Mary" *says Rebecca*

"Have you both settled into your new surroundings?" *asks Steve*

"Oh, yes we're at home here" *insists Mary*

"You know if there's anything we can do … anything at all just call" *says Steve*

"Oh, we will Steve, thank you for your kindness and generosity" *says Rebecca*

All leave and go into their respective office suites …

"Quite a dish, isn't he?" *says Mary*

"Remember who you are and why we are here" *advises Rebecca*

"Quite a dish indeed!" *responds Rebecca*

"Well … we are in human form after all Rebecca and it's ok to flirt" *advises Mary*

"Flirt?" *asks Rebecca*

"Oh, you know what I mean Rebecca" *says Mary*

"There is no harm in looking Mary ... but remember who we really are and why we are here" advises Rebecca

Meanwhile back at the Bar Convent, Nicola and John Paul have a situation to deal with ...

Someone from the Press has turned up investigating certain events that have transpired in the city of York ...

Nicola starts to panic ...

"Quick John Paul ... someone from the Press has arrived asking about a man who recently saved someone's life at the Rose of York public house" advises Nicola

"Why did they come here?" asks Nicola

"Don't worry Nicola I'll deal with the situation" advises John Paul

"It's time for a change of disguise to deal with this matter" says John Paul

John Paul turns into an older priest ...

Father McNeil ... an Irish priest from Dublin ...

The News reporter is shown into the Great Hall ...

"Good morning ... may I help you?" says a voice

"You must be Father McNeil?" asks the reporter

"Yes, I am, how can I help you?" advises the priest

"My name is John Flanagan" advises the reporter

"Well, how can I help you Mr. Flanagan?" asks the priest

"I have been directed here ... I am looking for a gentleman who saved a young womans life yesterday at the Rose of York pub" asks the reporter

"Directed here ... directed by whom?" asks the priest

"Well let's sa, I'm acting on a tip off" advises the reporter

"Well that all sounds very fascinating, but I fail to understand why you are here Mr Flanagan" advises the priest

"Who sent you and why did they send you?" asks the priest

"You're from the Newspapers … right?" asks the priest

"I am … the York Evening Post" advises Flanagan

"Maybe you've heard of us Father?" asks the reporter

"I'm sorry to inform you, there is no story here" insists the priest

"Who sent you?" asks the priest

"I have my sources" advises Flanagan

"Well, Mr Flanagan on this occasion your sources are wrong" advises the priest

"This is the Bar Convent we do not know of anything with regards to someone saving someone's life" advises the priest

"An angel … I was informed that an angel saved their life" advises Flanagan

"An angel?" asks the priest

"Really … how wonderful … but I am afraid you will not find any angels here … except the ones in the fine paintings about the convent" insists the priest

"Oh?" asks Flanagan

"I'm sorry … but there are no angels here … you've had a wasted journey" insists the priest

"Well, I'll leave my card … if you know of anything please get in touch" advises Flanagan

"I'll be sure to do that" says the priest

"Good day to you Mr. Flanagan" says the priest

"Good day Father …" says the reporter

"Perhaps if you go to the Minster" says the priest

The News reporter leaves the Bar Convent …

John Paul changes back into his own familiar appearance … and he advises Nicola of his brush with the press …

"What happened?" asks Nicola

"Don't worry ... situation averted. They accepted my story" says John Paul

"Then it's all over?" asks Nicola

"Well, I wouldn't say that ... but for now we're in the clear" advises John Paul

"We're still in control and cloaked in secrecy" informs John Paul

Back at Park Square in Leeds, Rebecca and Mary uncover another case after reading several files ...

"Well, what do you think to this case Mary? asks Rebecca

"It sounds like someone needs help fast" advises Mary

"I agree" responds Rebecca

"Who is it?" asks Mary

"A woman called Sian ... she's thinking of killing herself by train" says Rebecca

"Committing suicide?" asks Mary

"How do you know, Rebecca?" asks Mary

"A form of telepathy ... remember what Michael said ... nothing is above or below us" advises Rebecca

"... and it's going to happen soon if we don't get there fast Mary" insists Rebecca

"She's a client in need?" asks Mary

"Yes, in need urgently or it may be fatal" advises Rebecca

"How can we locate her?" asks Mary

"We will have to trust our instincts ... our heavenly grace and above all our vision of the future" advises Rebecca

"... and what does the future hold?" asks Mary

"We will find out when we locate Sian" advises Rebecca

"OK ... let's make tracks ... we must get there in time" insists Rebecca

Back at the Bar Convent, John Paul, and Nicola are summoned to help someone in distress on Lendal Bridge, which is in central York …

Joseph updates John Paul and Nicola about the possibility of a tragic suicide …

"*Why the rush Joseph?*" *asks John Paul*

"*Someone is threatening to jump from Lendal Bridge!*" *advises Joseph*

"*Can you help?*" *asks Joseph*

"*We'll do all we can Joseph … you know that*" *says Nicola*

"*It could be a matter of life and death*" *says Joseph*

"*OK lead the way Joseph*" *says John Paul*

Lendal Bridge is a famous Bridge in York. It is located near to the city centre and in walking distance of York Station and the Bar Walls close to the Minster

… The Bar Convent is also nearby …

The bridge is made of cast iron with stone structures at either side of the river Ouse …

Joseph, John-Paul, and Nicola arrive on the bridge where a crowd has now gathered …

The Police are now at the scene …

"*Stand back … please stand back*" *asks a police officer*

"*Maybe we can help?*" *asks Nicola*

"*Are you skilled in negotiations?*" *asks the officer*

"*Our skills are second to none*" *advises John Paul*

"*OK let them through*" *says another voice*

"*I'm Detective Sergeant Max Draper … do you think you can help?*" *asks Draper*

"*I'm John Paul … this is Nicola … we're skilled negotiators*" *advises John Paul*

"In what?" asks the detective

"Everything" responds Nicola

"Do you think you can talk him down?" asks Draper

"Well, we can try" advises Nicola

"The victim is male, about 45 years old" advises Draper

"What's his name officer?" asks John Paul

"Brian ... his name is Brian" advises Draper

"OK let's see what we can do" says John Paul

"Can you hear me, Brian?" asks John Paul

"Don't come any further or I will jump" advises Brian

"Don't jump Brian ... stay with me" advises John Paul

"Whatever for ... I have nothing to live for ... it is all over" insists Brian

"I'm coming closer" says John Paul

"Don't come any closer" warns Brian

"Does he know what he is doing? asks the detective

"Things can change Brian ... we can sort things out" says John Paul

"What are you doing?" asks Brian

"We only want to help" advises Nicola

"Then you can help me by going away" warns Brian

"Don't come any nearer" advises Brian

"Go away ... I am beyond help" says Brian

"It won't solve anything doing what you're doing" advises Nicola

"Keep hold on his attention Nicola ... I may have to try something" says John Paul

"Be very careful ... there are no safety nets on the bridge" says the detective

"No one can help me ... no one cares" says Brian

Nicola asks why this has happened and the detective gives her the full story …

"His wife, Pamela, advises it is due to business pressure and worries" says the detective

"Come back here to safety Brian … it is not worth throwing your life away … nothing is" advises John Paul

"I'm going to try something" says John Paul

"Be careful John Paul" says Nicola

More Police are now at the scene and the area has been cordoned off. Police negotiators are also there but the detective thinks John Paul has the way of turning things around …

"Hold on my orders … we're beginning to get somewhere" advises the detective

"Brian, think of your wife and children" asks John Paul

"They want to help you" advises John Paul

"We can save you" shouts Nicola

"Belief and faith are all you need" says John Paul

"Time's running out" says the detective

"It is getting cold Brian … your wife Pamela is here … come down so we can talk this over" asks John Paul

Brian is hesitant and he loses his footing on the bridge and almost falls …

"Stay where you are Brian … I am coming to get you" says John Paul

"Does he know what he's doing?" asks the detective

"John Paul is a skilled negotiator in these matters … trust him" advises Nicola

"OK … but we need to wrap this up" advises the detective

John Paul manages to reach Brian, who is now in the middle of Lendal bridge with the river Ouse below …

The river is calm, but it has hidden currents and it has claimed many who have fallen into it ...

"Hold on Brian ... I am there" says John Paul

"Don't look down ... keep your eyes fixed on me" says John Paul

"I don't think I can hold on much longer" says Brian

"Reach out and grab my hand" insists John Paul

"But we may both fall ..." says Brian

"Do you really believe Brian?" asks John Paul

"Just believe and you'll survive ... whatever happens" says John Paul

"I believe" says Brian

John Paul puts out his hand but Brian misses and both end up in the river ...

A couple of minutes pass then suddenly John Paul emerges with Brian and both are brought to safety by a Police launch ...

"That really was a close call" says the detective

"Are they both alright?" asks Nicola

"Yes, both are OK" advises the detective

"Are you OK Brian?" asks John Paul

"You see that's what you get when you trust, and you say you believe" says Brian

"Your here by the grace of God Brian" says Nicola

"Any longer in the river and you'd have caught pneumonia" advises a Police Officer

"So, you see Brian, God did save you" advises John Paul

"Anyway, Brian you agreed to talk ... are you ready to talk?" asks John Paul

"What here and now?" asks Brian

"There's no time like the present" advises John Paul

The motor launch pulls into the quay side of the river. There to greet Brian is Detective Sergeant Max Draper and Nicola …

"You were a brave man out there on the bridge, John Paul" advises the detective

"The crowds have got you down as a hero … what do you think to that?" asks the detective

"All part of the job Max … all part of the job" insists John Paul

"Well, I for one agree that you are good at what you do" says the detective

"Maybe we can work with you and Nicola again?" asks the detective

"Leave your details so we can get in touch" asks Draper

"We will" says Nicola

"OK I'm ready to talk" advises Brian

"How can you help me?" asks Brian

"It is a two-way thing Brian … let us guide you … we are not like others … we are not ordinary … trust in what we are saying" advises John Paul

"Max is there somewhere we can talk to Brian?" asks Nicola

"What about down the nick?" advises the detective

"No, that would be too formal" says John Paul

"I won't go there" insists Brian

"What about the café on the railway concourse at the museum?" says Max

"It's just a short walk from here" says the detective

"I don't want any fuss" says Brian

"OK … I will agree to that" says Brian

"We'll be in touch Brian" says the detective

Brian and his wife, Pamela, follow John Paul and Nicola to the café …

"Trust me Brian … I need you to trust me" asks John Paul

"OK I will trust you" advises Brian

"Give me your right hand" asks John Paul

Brian offers John Paul his right hand and a bright light begins to shine …

"What's happening?" asks Brian

"What have you done to me?" asks Brian

"You … you have saved me" insists Brian

"Your faith has saved you Brian" advises Nicola

"It's true your faith has saved you" says John Paul

"We're just glad to help" advises Nicola

"Who are you?" asks Brian

"Tell me who you really are so I can thank you?" asks Brian

"Oh, we are just passers-by who heard your cries for help" advises John Paul

"But I didn't make any cries for help" pleads Brian

"God heard you" advises Nicola

"God?" asks Brian

"Just be grateful that we have managed to help you … now go and live your life" advises John Paul

"Who are you?" asks Brian

"Angels, Brian … we are both Angels" advises John Paul

"Real angels?" asks Brian

"Yes, real angels … tell no one what has happened" asks Nicola

"Remember to keep our secret" says Nicola

"Now … we must go" advises John Paul

"Go where?" asks Brian

"Thank you" says Brian

In a flash Nicola and John Paul have left the area …

"Do you think he will keep our secret?" asks Nicola

"I've made it so that he will not remember anything" advises John Paul

"The only thing he will remember is being saved but he won't remember why" advises John Paul

Back in Leeds, Rebecca and Mary arrive just in time to save Sian from throwing herself under a train …

The incident was taking place on a busy train line out of Morley into Leeds.

Various Pennine Express trains go through the busy station regularly. Luckily, Rebecca and Mary arrive before the next train is due …

"Are you alright Sian?" asks Mary

Sian is a middle-aged woman; she has fair hair and green eyes …

"I don't know why I decided to do that?" advises Sian

"Please don't ever do that again" asks Rebecca

"Your life is very important" advises Mary

"Why did you stop me?" asks Sian

"God told us to" advises Rebecca

"God?" asks Sian

"Who are you?" asks Sian

"We're angels … your guardian angels" advises Rebecca

"How did you know I was planning to commit suicide?" asks Sian

"God knows everything" advises Mary

"Tell no one of what's happened" says Rebecca

"Thank you … I am so happy you saved me" says Sian

"Promise that you'll never attempt to do it again" asks Rebecca

"Yes, I promise" advises Sian

"You are happy because you can see us" says Mary

"There are many who can't see and yet believe" says Rebecca

"I was a whisker away from killing myself" says Sian

"I was close to death" insists Sian

"Yes, you were ... now you have been saved ... we are only partakers in God's work" advises Rebecca

"Is God's Kingdom far?" asks Sian

"The Kingdom of God is here within you ... now" advises Rebecca

"I promise I will follow all the days of my life" advises Sian

"We must go now Sian" advises Mary

"Go ... go where?" asks Sian

"There are many more lives we need to save" advises Rebecca

"Our work is never over ... we must go to our next assignment" advises Mary

"But if anyone asks me who sent you ... what shall I tell them?" asks Sian

"Tell them I am sent us ... that's all you need to say" advises Rebecca

Both Rebecca and Mary leave the scene in a flash ...

Sian is now back on the station platform ...

The Station Master asks if she is all right ...

Sian begins to tell her story ...

A Pennine Express train thunders through the station and rattles the platform ...

It is not long before reporters from the Yorkshire Evening Post arrive on the concourse ...

They start to question Sian ...

"What happened?" asks the reporter

Sian starts to relate her story …

The more the Reporters question Sian the more they disprove her story …

"But it's all true, angels really did save me today" insists Sian

"What evidence have we to say so?" asks the reporter

Sian points to the spot where white feathers have been found …

"So it's all true?" asks the reporter

"White feathers appear when angels are near"

SAVED BY THE BELL

A tragedy in York averted. Ghostly goings on at Leeds General Infirmary. The York Maze. Looking for Martha. Save my little girl. The Gray Lady. Mission and phenomenon …

Dilemma and tragedy form part of this story.

Can the Angels avert a catastrophe in York?

Back in Leeds there are "ghostly" goings on at the General Infirmary!

The Bar Convent, York … John Paul and Peter are in conversation about an attraction just outside of the city …

"What's all this hype about the York Maze, Peter?" asks John Paul

"It sounds amazing … sorry for the pun!" says Nicola

"Oh, it is John Paul … it's a kind of game … you start at the beginning and try to find the middle but there are twists and turns at every corner. If you take the wrong way you could end up completely lost" advises Peter

"It is just like life Peter; a lot of people seem to end up lost taking the wrong road" says Nicola

"I agree" says John Paul

"We must see this maze" insists Nicola

"We can go later today if you wish?" asks Peter

A few hours later Peter arrives with Nicola and John Paul ...

The York Maze is a giant and one of the largest in Europe. It has a contemporary design every year for tourists to puzzle and solve.

You can come face to face with giant dinosaurs in the Jurassic Maze and watch shows and games taking place in the Crazy Maze. There are so many attractions to keep you on your toes there.

During the day, the slightly less intense Maze is aimed at the younger age groups.

They encounter a problem at the entrance ...

A young mum is in tears ...

"What's the problem?" asks Peter

"Oh, my little girl ... she's only tiny" advises the young woman

"What's happened to her?" asks John Paul

"I told her not to wander off ... I only took my eyes off her for a minute but when I turned around, she had gone" advises the young woman

"I think she has wandered into the maze, while I was purchasing our tickets" says the young woman

"Can you help me?" asks the young mum

"What's her name?" asks Nicola

"Oh, Martha ... she's called Martha ... she's only six" advises the young mum

"Can you describe her for us?" asks John Paul

"She has long golden hair ... blue eyes, wearing a pink dress" says the young mum

"OK ... sorry what's your name?" asks Nicola

"Oh, Clair" advises the young mum

"What's your names?" asks Clair

"That is Nicola and Peter … I am John Paul"

"Are you the Police or detectives?" asks Clair

"Sort of" advises John Paul

"OK Clair, this is what we'll do" insists John Paul

"Try not to panic" advises Nicola

"Both Nicola and I will go in search for Martha with Peter" says John Paul

"She's only little" says Clair

"Try not to worry" advises Nicola

"We'll bring her back safe and sound … try and keep calm" says John Paul

John Paul, Nicola, and Peter enter the maze …

After a short walk they encounter the Corn snake Tower Slides …

"Peter, you go left with Nicola … I will go right" advises John Paul

Peter and Nicola check the side area but there is no sign of Martha …

Similarly, John Paul checks the utter cornage and angry crow section without finding any trace of Martha …

"I wonder if John Paul has found any trace of Martha" asks Peter

"I would have known by now" says Nicola

"How?" asks Peter

"A form of telepathy" informs Nicola

"Really?" asks Peter

John Paul returns, advising the Park Rangers are now involved in the search for Martha …

"We have closed off the Park until further notice" advises a Ranger

"We've checked the first two sections" advises John Paul

"I doubt whether she will have wandered far" says the Ranger

"We'll move on to the cornwall section" says Nicola

"I will check out the Volcorno maze" advises John Paul

"We've also got other rangers checking the entire complex" advises the Ranger

After a long search of the cornwall section, Nicola and Peter locate Martha ... but she is not breathing ...

John Paul re-joins Nicola and Peter ...

"Don't tell me " says Peter

"Another form of telepathy?" advises Peter

"Yes ... absolutely" says Nicola

"Nicola ... both you and I will lay our hands on Martha" says John Paul

"What will that do?" asks Peter

"Watch and learn Peter" advises John Paul

A glowing bright light radiates from the angels and both touch on Martha's tiny frame ...

"Rise little girl" advises John Paul

... and at that command Martha begins to breathe and sits up, slightly dazed.

"That's amazing ... but how did you do it?" asks Peter

Nicola whispers to John Paul ...

"We may need to erase Peter's memory of what

just happened" advises Nicola

"I agree" advises John Paul

John Paul touches Peter on the arm and the whole incident is erased from his memory.

Peter cannot remember anything except for the joy of finding Martha alive and well.

John Paul, Nicola, and Peter return to the entrance where Martha's mum is waiting …

Clair is ecstatic with delight and crying at the same time …

"Oh, thank you, how can I thank you?" asks Clair

"By taking care of your little girl … she was so brave" says Nicola

"Sorry, what did you say your names were?" asks Clair

"Oh, we are so glad to have helped you … I am sent us" advises John Paul

"Who?" asks Clair

In a flash both Nicola and John *Paul with Peter have left the maze averting*

another tragedy.

However, back in York centre news of their good deed starts to spread of how they saved a little girls life at the Maze.

At the offices of The York Evening Post news comes in of their story …

"It's another unexplained happening … this time at the York Maze" says the Editor

"… but we're in luck this time" says a reporter

"What do you mean?" asks the Editor

"CCTV cameras are all over the maze area … we can find out who they really are" advises Mike Hanson

Mike Hanson is an experienced Journalist having worked in Leeds and York for the past 20 years …

"OK Mike … we need to see those tapes and what they throw up" says the Editor

"On to it … I have been in touch with my contact at the Maze … the tapes are being delivered here to us, as we speak" advises Mike

A junior worker brings in the tapes …

"Thanks Giles" advises the Editor

Mike puts on the tapes and starts to view their content …

"I don't believe it" says Mike

"What?" asks the Editor

"I can only see one man in the picture … where are the other two?" says Mike

"Are you sure you got it right Mike?" asks the Editor

"My contact specifically said there were three of them?" advises Mike

"Maybe they were wrong?" asks the Editor

"Maybe" advises Mike

"I'll go and talk to them later" says Mike

"Well, whatever happened it is another unexplained and unsolved mystery … but it is still an exceptional story" says the Editor

"We'll run it today" advises the Editor

Meanwhile, back in Leeds, Rebecca and Mary are looking into a file of ghostly goings on at the Leeds General Infirmary …

Park Square office suite, second floor …

"I've read the file Kate" says Rebecca

"What about you Mary?" asks Kate

"Yes, I have read it too" advises Mary

"What conclusions have you made from the file" asks Rebecca

"Conclusions?" asks Mary

"What are your thoughts in this matter?" asks Rebecca

"Well, I'm not really sure" replies Mary

"Who was the Gray lady?" asks Rebecca

"Apparently she regularly walks the wards at Leeds General Infirmary" says Kate

"Who was she?" asks Mary

"No one really knows but they think she may have been a nurse or

Ward sister there at some time in her life" advises Kate

"We must check this out Mary" says Rebecca

"Maybe we can help … maybe she is a lost soul" says Rebecca

"How can you help?" asks Kate

"Oh, we've come across this kind of phenomenon before" advises Mary

"You could say we are experts in our field with regards this kind of matter" advises Mary

"Second to none, I would say" advises Rebecca

"Can I come with you on this one?" asks Kate

"We usually work alone" says Rebecca

"It would be purely as an advisor" replies Kate

"Ok you can, but just as an observer" replies Rebecca

Kate leaves the office and gathers her things together …

Mary and Rebecca share their concerns about Kate at the Infirmary …

"Are you sure that was a good idea?" asks Mary

"Well, if Kate does see anything … we can erase that moment from her memory… and she would give us extra cover" advises Rebecca

"OK Rebecca I agree" replies Mary

Kate returns to the meeting room …

"OK Rebecca let's check out the Gray Lady" says Mary

"Kate … we agree you can help us too" advises Rebecca

"Yes … I would love to" says Kate enthusiastically

All three walk out of their suite in Park Square and cross the busy Headrow towards St. Annes's Cathedral. They continue to walk over Milennium Square up the hill towards the Jubilee Wing of Leeds General Infirmary …

"Can I help you?" asks a male receptionist

"Oh, we are investigators and we have been assigned to investigate the paranormal things that have been happening here" advises Rebecca

"Paranormal?" asks the receptionist

"Oh, you mean The Gray Lady ... she's part of the furniture here" advises the male receptionist

"Part of the furniture?" asks Mary

"It's just a way of saying Mary ... everyone here is aware of her existence" advises Kate

"Well, we've come to see for ourselves" says Rebecca

"Yes, where can we find her? asks Mary

"Follow me" says the male receptionist

"She is said to haunt the upper floors between Wards 10 and 14 ... you may have a bit of a wait though" advises the male receptionist

"Why?" asks Mary

"It's usually from 8pm onwards" advises the male receptionist

"That's over two hours" says Kate

"Well, you can set up in here if you want to" advises the male receptionist

"Set up?" asks Mary

"Set up what?" asks Rebecca

"You're recording equipment of course ... I presume you have that with you? asks the male receptionist

"Well?" replies Mary

"Actually, we don't have any recording equipment" advises Rebecca

"Well how do you plan to expose the Gray lady?" asks the male receptionist

"By calling her out of course" says Mary

"Calling her out?" asks the male receptionist

"It's a bit primitive isn't it love?" advises the male receptionist

"Anyway, I will leave you all here … if it gets a bit scary call out or phone me at reception "says the male receptionist

"Ask for Tom" says the male receptionist

"Thanks Tom" says Rebecca

Tom heads back down to reception …

"Bit of a blokey bloke, wasn't he?" advises Mary

"Blokey bloke?" asks Rebecca

"You know … a man's man" says Mary

"We do now Mary" laughs Kate

"You never fail to amuse me, Mary" advises Rebecca

"You were spot on though Mary" says Kate

"Blokey Bloke indeed" laughs Rebecca

Just over two hours later when the clock strikes 8 sure enough the form of a ghostly apparition comes into view …

The figure of the Gray Lady appears …

Rebecca stands in her way and asks a question …

"Who are you" asks Rebecca

"Why are you here?" asks Mary

"You are both angels" says the Gray Lady

"We have been sent for you" advises Rebecca

"Why were you sent for me?" asks the Gray Lady

"I've got a job to do here at the Infirmary" replies the Gray Lady

Mary becomes anxious …

"Is Kate with you Rebecca?" asks Mary

"No … I am here … I thought there was something different about you two" replies Kate

"You will have to keep our secret Kate" advises Mary

"What do you want of me?" asks the Gray Lady

"We need to take you home ..." advises Rebecca

"Why didn't you go down the tunnel into the light? asks Rebecca

"My work is here" says the Gray Lady

"You have no work here" advises Rebecca

"Please follow the road before you into heaven ... before it's too late" advises Rebecca

A white swirling tunnel opens before them in the corridor and a bright light awaits at the end of it ...

"Your family are waiting for you" advises Mary

"My family?" asks the Gray Lady

"Yes ... now make haste and follow the road before your trapped here forever" says Rebecca

"But what about my work?" asks the Gray Lady

"We will carry on your work for you" advises Rebecca

"I'm afraid" advises the Gray Lady

"No need to be ... now hurry" says Rebecca

The Gray Lady starts to enter the white swirling tunnel and can see people moving about on the other side ...

She leaves this world and enters the next ...

Mary touches Kate advising that her memory of what has just happened will disappear and that she will only remember her visit to the Infirmary.

"What happened?" asks Kate

"Don't you remember ... we're at the General Infirmary?" advises Mary

"Why am I at the Infirmary?" asks Kate

HEAVENLY SENT

When a Loan Shark starts to prey on the innocent in York … John Paul, and Nicola come to their aid … back in Leeds, Rebecca and Mary are investigating into mending broken hearts and Speed Dating!

John Paul and Nicola are reaffirming their commitment to the investigation's in York and are in conversation at the Bar Convent …

"Believe in something … even if it means sacrificing everything" advises John Paul

"Maybe, we have already sacrificed everything John Paul?" replies Nicola

"Yes, but do you believe Nicola … do you really believe?" asks John Paul

"Naturally, I do … I wholeheartedly do in everything and all that we are doing here on Earth" replies Nicola

"Well, do you think we are successfully carrying out God's message, and instructions?" asks John Paul

"Yes of course, don't you?" asks Nicola

"I truly believe Nicola" advises John Paul

"And … we must leave a lasting legacy" insists John Paul

"I agree" advises Nicola

"I think we have already made our impression with regards to that matter" advises John Paul

"Do you think Michael would approve?" asks Nicola

"Oh, I'm sure he's proud of what we're doing here" replies John Paul

Peter enters the room with several files for the angels to look over …

"Well, Peter … what have we got this time?" asks John Paul

"What have you found?" asks Nicola

"We have been approached by several people concerning a Loan Shark who is praying on the lives of ordinary men and women, and in particular a lady named Maxine, who is looking for our help" replies Peter

"A loan shark … praying?" asks Nicola

"What do you mean?" asks John Paul

"A loan shark is someone who loans money to people, then extorts payment at a massive percentage … they are the lowest of the low" says Peter

"Indeed, they are" agrees John Paul

"We must see how we can help Maxine" advises Nicola

"You may need to set a trap" advises Peter

"Set a trap?" asks Nicola

"We're not into that type of business" advises John Paul

"Oh, now I understand" says John Paul

"What Peter means is that we may need to draw them out into the open Nicola" advises John Paul

"Now I understand too" advises Nicola

"Exactly … that's what needs to be done" confirms Peter

"Do you have Maxine's address?" asks Nicola

"She lives across the city, in a block of flats" advises Peter

"We must go there at once" advises John Paul

"We look forward to meeting this loan shark" says Nicola

Back in Leeds, Mary and Rebecca are investigating into mending broken hearts!

Park Square, 2nd floor, angel investigation's office suite …

"What has an angel got to do?" asks Mary

"I don't follow Mary?" advises Rebecca

Mary continues to extract information from several files and puts over the stories to Rebecca …

"Well Rebecca, it seems there are a lot of broken hearts in Leeds" advises Mary

"Broken hearts?" asks Rebecca

"What do you mean, Mary? questions Rebecca

"I have just read an advertisement for Speed Dating … it says it will mend your broken heart" advises Mary

"Speed Dating?" puzzles Rebecca

"We must learn more about this" advises Rebecca

"What else does it say?" asks Rebecca

"Does it say where we should go for Speed Dating?" asks Rebecca

Mary continues to check into the advertisement …

"The advertisement says the next one is being held at the Metropole Hotel in the centre of Leeds" advises Mary

Kate enters the meeting …

"We were just discussing the possibility of Speed Dating" advises Mary

"Speed dating?" asks Kate

"Where?" asks Kate

"Here in the centre of Leeds, at the Metropole Hotel … do you know it?" asks Rebecca

"The Metropole Hotel is not far from here and we can get to it on foot" advises Kate

"OK Kate … are you coming with us to investigate into this phenomenon?" asks Mary

"Oh, yes I'm intrigued too" laughs Kate

"But, it's not a phenomenon" advises Kate

"Well, what is it all about Kate?" asks Mary

"You really don't know do you?" says Kate

"Well, no …not really … please explain" asks Rebecca

"Well, I'm no expert, but this is basically what happens …" advises Kate

"Go on" asks Mary

"There will be several tables for you to sit at" advises Kate

"You will get a few minutes at each table with a potential blind date … if you like them, you exchange phone numbers and other details … that is how it is done" advises Kate

"Why are they blind?" asks Mary

"No, they are not blind … it is called a blind date because you have only just met them" laughs Kate

"I don't get it" puzzles Rebecca

"It all sounds very peculiar … now back in my day" says Mary

"That is quite enough about back in your day Mary … we must try this Speed dating ourselves" advises Rebecca

"Well, OK, it's on tonight" advises Kate

"We will all go Kate!" advises Mary

Back in York, Nicola and John Paul arrive at Maxine's flat which is just on the outskirts of the city …

After negotiating several flights of stairs, they knock on the door …

"Hello … we're Nicola and John Paul … this is Peter … we're from the agency" says Nicola

"I believe you need our help?" asks John Paul

"Hi … I am Maxine … yes indeed I do" advises Maxine

"How can we help you, Maxine?" asks Nicola

"I've got myself in debt to a loan shark" advises Maxine

"How much do you owe?" asks Nicola

"Just over a thousand pounds at the last count but he is now trying to extract five thousand pounds for the loan" advises Maxine

"Is he now" says John Paul

"OK, phone and tell him … tell him you want to see him … now" advises Nicola

"Yes, we need to draw him out into the open" insists John Paul

"What's happening?" asks Peter

"What do you want me to do?" says Peter

"Don't worry we will capture this tiger by the tail" says John Paul

"Just believe and it will happen" says Nicola

John Paul and Nicola leave Peter with Maxine promising to return later …

They leave the block of flats …

"Time to change our disguise" advises John Paul

An hour later … Zac the loan shark arrives at Maxine's flat …

"Well, what do you want … have you got my money?" asks the loan shark

"No, she hasn't but we have" advises John Paul and Nicola now disguised as Police officers …

"Your nicked" advises John Paul

"For what?" asks the loan shark

"Extortion … and you will give this lady back all you have taken from her now" insists Nicola

"On what authority?" asks the loan shark

"On God's authority ... now pay the lady" advises Nicola

John Paul holds the loan shark by the throat and raises him off the ground by a couple of feet ...

The loan shark squeals ...

"OK, OK ... here's the money" advises the loan shark

Maxine and Peter go back into the flat with the money owed ...

"You will remember nothing about this Zac" advises John Paul

"If you carry on your unscrupulous deeds, you will face unreversible consequences" advises Nicola

"Oh, I promise" says the loan shark

John Paul and Nicola let Zac go ... they then change back into their normal look ...

Back at Maxine's flat there is a certain amount of relief with regards the loan shark ...

"Your troubles are over Maxine" advises John Paul

"What about Zac?" asks Maxine

"Don't worry, he won't bother you again" advises John Paul

"What happened?" asks Peter

"Let's just say he has seen the error of his ways" says Nicola

"You see Peter all it needed was a little gentle persuasion" advises John Paul

"But I saw nothing ... how did you do it?" asks Peter

Back in Leeds, Rebecca, Mary, and Kate enter The Metropole Hotel ahead of the Speed Dating evening ...

The Metropole Hotel is a Grade 2 listed building situated on King Street in the heart of Leeds. It opened in 1899 and it is built of a rare and remarkable Terracotta façade ...

Inside The Grand Ball room ...

"Looks like this is the place Kate" says Mary

"Yes, this is it" advises Kate

"What do you think of it?" asks Kate

"So far so good" says Rebecca

Someone on the door of the Grand Ball room steps forward ...

"Are you ladies here to partake in the Speed Dating event?" asks a young man

"Yes, I believe we are" says Mary

"May I show you to your table?" asks the young man

"Yes, why not?" says Kate

"Please follow me ... this way" advises the young man

The Grand Ball room is starting to fill up with love struck hopefuls filling up all the available tables ...

The Event organiser steps in and announces that the evening is open ...

"When we ring the bell, you will have about 10 minutes to impress those at the your table, then when we ring it again you move on to the next table" advises the organiser

"That's all there is to it?" asks Mary

"It doesn't sound too complicated" says Rebecca

Someone rings the bell, and the Speed dating begins ...

"Hi, my name is Rebecca ... and you are?" asks Rebecca

"Oh, Martin ... I am Martin" says a good-looking young man

"Where are you from?" asks Martin

"Oh, Leeds ... and you?" replies Rebecca

"Well, far away from here" advises Mary

"What are you looking for?" asks Rebecca

"Something out of the ordinary" replies Martin

"Maybe we can help you" replies Mary

"We?" asks Martin

"Oh, we come as a pair" responds Mary

"A pair?" asks Martin

"I've come here with Mary and Kate" says Rebecca

"Wow … I cannot believe my luck" responds Martin

"What's luck got to do with it?" asks Rebecca

The bell rings … everyone moves on to the next table …

"Hello … my name is James" says a voice

"Hello … my name is Rebecca"

"What do you think about devolution?" asks James

"That was not a question I was expecting at speed dating" replies Rebecca

"Sorry I'm nervous" advises James

"Don't be" says Mary

"What do you think about angels?" asks Rebecca

"Do you know any?" asks James

"You're talking to one" advises Mary

The bell rings again … everyone moves again to the next table …

"Hi … I am Peter" says a voice

"Hello, my name is Rebecca … where are you from Peter?"

"Oh, York … with John Paul and Nicola" says Peter

"Peter, what are you doing here?" laughs Rebecca

"Is this a joke?" asks Mary

"No, they are here … right behind you" advises Peter

John Paul and Nicola are standing and wave …

"When is it your turn girls?" asks John Paul

"We're waiting for our slot" advises Kate

Rebecca leaves the floor and re-joins Kate and Mary …

"Well, this is a surprise" advises John Paul

"… and what is the meaning of all this John-Paul?" asks Rebecca

"We thought we would come and surprise you" says Nicola

"Well, it's great fun this speed dating" advises Rebecca

Mary and Kate now take up their slots on the table …

"We've got another case for you" advises John Paul

"Another case?" asks Mary

"It's heaven sent" advises Nicola

"That's right … we're all needed on this one" says John Paul

"When do we start?" asks Rebecca

"Straight away" advises Nicola

"What do we have this time?" asks Mary

"A jumper in a car park … not far from here" says John Paul

"How do you know?" asks Rebecca

"Michael advised us" advises John Paul

Rebecca signals to Mary and Kate to come and join them …

"Just when I was enjoying myself" says Mary

"We've been summoned by Michael" advises Rebecca

"Where are we going?" asks Mary

"Someone needs our help straight away" says John Paul

"Where?" asks Mary

"Follow me" advises John Paul

GOD'S MESSENGERS – A BLESSING IN DISGUISE

A meeting of the Press raises suspicion! The Angel's encounter beggars on the street in modern day Leeds. They also must deal with more broken lives, a honeytrap, being mistaken and an identity check!

Park Square, Leeds, Angel's Investigations, 2nd floor private suite ... early morning ...

"We have received a request from the York Evening Post and the Evening Post in Leeds for a meeting asking why and what Angel's means" advises Kate

"Do you think they are setting a trap?" asks Mary

"Yes, it could be a way of trapping us" advises Nicola

"What do you think John Paul?" asks Rebecca

"No, I think it is just a formality" advises John Paul

"When are they asking to meet us?" asks John Paul

"This week" advises Kate

"What shall I tell them?" asks Kate

"Advise both newspapers that we will all meet here at our Park Square offices in Leeds … we will be ready when they arrive" advises John Paul

"Do we all agree?" asks John Paul

"Yes, I think we should be open so that they can see we have nothing to hide" advises Rebecca

Meanwhile. later in the city centre Mary and Rebecca encounter a different problem … beggars on the street!

Merrion Centre, Leeds in the heart of the city centre …

"Why?" asks Mary

"Why on earth are people begging in the street?" asks Mary

"It's a modern-day crisis" advises Kate

"You mean it's just allowed for people to beg?" asks Rebecca

"Well, now it is … but the government have promised to eradicate it everywhere in the next few years" advises Kate

"How exactly?" asks Mary

"Mm … Politicians … full of promises … but will it ever happen? asks Rebecca

"We must meet some of these beggars today Kate, and end their plight" advises Mary

"Well, OK but …" says Kate

"No ifs or buts, take us to them now" insists Rebecca

A short walk from the Merrion Centre, Kate, Rebecca and Mary encounter their first beggar …

"Hello pretty lady … spare some change?" asks a beggar

Kate rustles in her handbag and hands over a few pounds …

"Why are you begging?" asks Mary

"I have nowhere to go" is the response

"Don't you have a family?" asks Rebecca

"Oh … Mac is my only family" says the beggar

"Mac?" asks Rebecca

"Oh, my dog" advises the beggar

"Give him some more money Kate" asks Rebecca

"OK Rebecca but …" says Kate

"You won't like it when I tell you" insists Kate

"What do you mean?" asks Rebecca

"Oh, he's a professional beggar" advises Kate

"A professional beggar in what way?" asks Mary

"He is well known in the city … he comes into Leeds by train, he has got his own house in the suburbs … and he is well known to the Police!" advises Kate

"Is this true?" asks Mary

The beggar remains silent …

"Well, is it true?" asks Rebecca

"Yes, I am afraid it is" replies the beggar

"Why do you do it?" asks Mary

"Modern day phenomenon … it beats working!" replies the beggar

"Your unscrupulous" says Mary

"You're not vulnerable at all" responds Rebecca

"See I told you that you wouldn't like it" advises Kate

"Are there any more like him?" asks Mary

"Yes … but it's hard to tell which ones" advises Kate

"Not for us" insists Rebecca

"We will have to deal with this modern-day phenomenon" advises Mary

"That will have to wait" advises Kate

"Why?" asks Rebecca

"John Paul and Nicola … have you forgotten your meeting with the press?" advises Kate

"OK, we must leave" says Rebecca

"You're a lucky man … today you escaped but tomorrow will come and we will meet you again …" says Rebecca

"If we do, we will have no choice but to …" advises Mary

"Careful Rebecca … remember what Michael said" says Mary

"OK, we will deal with it another way … until tomorrow" advises Mary

Meanwhile, John Paul, Nicola and Peter await the arrival of Mary, Rebecca, and Kate at the Park Square office suite …

"The press is due to arrive any minute" advises Nicola

"Remember, we must all be very careful of our responses" says John Paul

"I suspect they will be digging and delving … you can be sure of that" says John Paul

"We must use our intuition and be discreet and open at all times" says Nicola

"Let the truth be known … but only if it needs to be told" advises John Paul

"Above all remember what Michael said" advises Rebecca

The Press from York and Leeds arrive on time and are shown into the

Angel's office suite …

"Can I offer you some tea or coffee?" asks Kate

"Make mine a strong cup of tea" says a reporter

"I will have a black coffee" says another reporter

"I'm Mike Jarvis … this is my associate Jack Irving from York" says the reporter

"Now gentlemen you must have a lot of questions … how can we help you?" asks John Paul

Kate enters the room and hands out the tea and coffee …

"Thank you" say the reporters

"So, tell me … where did you come from?" asks Mike Jarvis

"And … who set up Angel's Investigations?" asks Jack Irving

"What does Angel's mean?" asks Jack Irving

"And have you anything to do with the recent miracles in the city?" asks Mike Jarvis

"Miracles?" asks Rebecca

"We don't know anything about miracles" says John Paul

"Are you miracle workers?" asks Mike

"We would have to be God to work miracles" replies Nicola

"Then you aren't God?" asks Jack

"No … of course not" says Rebecca

"We merely help people with broken lives … help those in distress in any way we can, that is our goal" responds Mary

"What about you Kate, have you anything to say?" asks Mike

"All investigations are client based, although sometimes we do get requests by phone" replies Kate

"Really gentlemen if we were miracle workers we would have been found out by now" responds John Paul

"We are happy to talk about the investigations we have done ... if that is what you are interested in" advises Rebecca

"Are you God's messengers ... a blessing in disguise?" asks Jack

"We help others in distress in any way we can ... that's what we do" replies Nicola

"That's all you do?" asks Mike

"We simply investigate and solve problems for anyone asking for our help" advises John Paul

"Do you have any special powers?" asks Jack

"The only power we have is through faith and belief" advises Rebecca

"If you have faith and belief ... you have everything" says Mary

"Well, gentlemen do you have any other questions?" asks John Paul

Mike and Jack look at each other then agree ...

"Thank you for your time ... is it OK if we contact you again?" asks Mike

"Feel free to do so ... please advise Kate" advises John Paul

Both Mike and Jack leave the Angel's suite ...

"I think we took care of that situation quite well, don't you?" says Rebecca

"Well, we may have satisfied their curiosity for now" says John Paul

"Why do you say that, John Paul?" asks Nicola

"I've got a feeling that we will be seeing them again" advises John Paul

Meanwhile, Mike Jarvis and Jack Irving are now seated at a bar near to Park Square discussing the meeting ...

"Well, what do you think Jack?" asks Mike

"There's something they are hiding" advises Jack

"Yes ... I think your right" insists Mike

"Maybe if we devise a plan to draw them out into the open?" advises

Mike

"What have you got in mind?" asks Jack

"A honey trap ... maybe we can draw John Paul into it?" advises Mike

"OK ... we'll never know if we don't try it" says Jack

Jack Irving and Mike are given the green light to spring a trap and are given full backing by their respective newspapers ...

A few days later a phone call to Angel's Eyes Investigations reveals a decoy has been set up as bait to draw them out into the open ...

The phone rings in reception ...

"Angel's Eyes Investigations ... how may I help you?" asks Kate

"Hello ... may I speak to John Paul?" says a voice

"Who is calling?" asks Kate

"My name is Caroline ... I am a victim of abuse" says the voice

"What kind of abuse?" asks Kate

"I've been beaten repeatedly by my husband ... can you help me?" asks Caroline

"Hold the line ... I will put you through to John Paul" advises Kate

John Paul's phone rings ... "John Paul" asks Kate

"Hello John Paul ... I've a lady called Caroline asking for our help ... it sounds like domestic abuse" advises Kate

"OK Kate, I will take it from here ... put her through" advises John Paul

"John Paul here ... how may I help you?" responds John Paul

"My name is Caroline. I have been repeatedly beaten by my husband can you help me?" asks Caroline

"Have you contacted the Police?" asks John Paul

"Not yet" advises Caroline

"I suggest you contact them first ... I am on my way" assures John Paul

"What's your address?" asks John Paul

"I'm in Cardigan Road, just outside the city" advises Caroline

Peter and Nicola enter John Paul's office and he updates them …

"Peter and Nicola, you closely follow behind just in case I need your help" advises John Paul

All three jump into a waiting taxi …

"Where to?" asks the Driver

"Cardigan Road … do you know it?" asks John Paul

"Yea I know it … I was brought up near the Headingly Cricket Ground" advises the taxi driver

The taxi arrives at Cardigan Road within a matter of minutes …

"What's the exact location?" asks the driver

"It's OK, drop us all off here, we'll walk the rest of the way" says John Paul

Peter pays the taxi driver …

"OK … be vigilant … there's something not right with this investigation" advises John Paul

"How do you know?" asks Nicola

"Remember our sixth sense?" advises John Paul

"Well, mine just kicked in" says John Paul

John Paul and the team arrive on the scene, but just has he predicted there is no one in distress …

"You come to meet me?" says a voice

"Who are you?" asks John Paul

"You're an angel, aren't you?" says the voice

"What do you want?" asks John Paul

"If you're an angel … show me your powers …, how do you do it?" asks the voice

"Do what?" asks John Paul

"Don't come too close" advises the voice

At that point, Nicola and Peter intervene ...

"What's going on?" asks Peter

"A trap ... I suspect set by the newspapers" says John Paul

"You've achieved nothing, we're not who you think we are" advises Nicola

"Mistaken ... you've mistaken us for who you are really looking for" advises John Paul

"If you're not who you say you are, then prove it" says the voice

"We don't have to ... there is nothing to prove" advises John Paul

"Can't you see there is no story here" says John Paul

"You'll have to try harder next time" advises Nicola

"Next time?" asks the reporter

"If there is a next time" advises Nicola

The Press begin to retreat, still convinced that a story is there ...

"We'll see what we can find" adds the reporter

Mike and Jack are in the background ...

"Well, what did you find out?" asks an Editor

"Nothing" advises Mike

"I still don't believe their story" says the Editor

"We must keep looking for the truth" advises Jack

BETWEEN THE LIVING AND THE DEAD

A healing takes place at Leeds City Railway Station. Rebecca, Mary, and Kate visit Samantha and investigate her powers. The

York Dungeon is check out by John Paul and Nicola. Ghostly apparitions and encounters with Roman soldiers. A meeting with the Centurian. Suspicion awakened. Bleeding heart statue in the Cathedral. Another brush with the Press. York Minster encounter. The Torchlight Procession, healing, and investigation ...

Leeds City Station ... approximately 10am, Monday morning, Rebecca is on her way to Park Square in the city centre when suddenly she is met with a problem on arrival at the station concourse ...

"Can you hear me, Melanie?" asks a young man

A crowd of train passengers gather round to help ...

Somone suddenly asks ... "Is there anything we can do?"

"I have made a mobile call .... and been told the ambulance and responder are on their way" advises the young man

A few minutes later the NHS responder arrives ...

"OK ... what happened ... have you made the victim comfortable?" asks the responder

"She just seemed to fall ... I have made her as comfortable as I can" advises the young man

Rebecca now enters the scene ...

"What's happened ... are you her knight in shining armour?" asks Rebecca

"Are you related to this lady?" asks the responder

"No ... sorry I'm not" advises Rebecca

"What's her name?" asks the responder

"Melanie ... her name is Melanie" advises the young man

"Can you hear me, Melanie?" asks the responder

"I need to get some more equipment from my vehicle. The ambulance is on its way ... nod if you understand?" asks the responder

Melanie nods ...

"OK I'll be back in a few minutes … sorry what's your name?" asks the responder

"Josh … my name is Josh" advises the young man

"OK Josh … I am Martin … back in few minutes" advises the responder

Rebecca steps forward to help …

"Melanie, can you hear me … I am going to help you?" advises Rebecca

"Can you help Melanie?" asks Josh

"Yes … nod if you understand Melanie … do you believe?" asks Rebecca

"My name is Rebecca … I can help you" advises Rebecca

Melanie nods her head …

Rebecca places her hands on Melanie …

"I'm going to lay my hands on you Melanie and you will feel a warm glow" advises Rebecca

"Do you understand Melanie?" asks Rebecca

"What are you doing?" asks Josh

"Is it a new type of medicine?" asks Josh

"Yes … but we need to be quick" insists Rebecca

Rebecca places both of her hands on Melanie and a warm bright light radiates from her … within a matter of seconds Melanie is healed and sitting up again …

The crowd are astonished to witness what has just happened …

The NHS responder returns with more equipment …

He finds Melanie sitting up and breathing normally …

"My God what happened … your OK?" asks the responder

"A lady helped me … she was an angel in disguise" says Melanie

"An angel?" asks the responder

"A blinding white light radiated from her ... she healed me ... I am alive" advises Melanie

"Where is this lady ... I must thank her?" insists Melanie

The NHS responder is astonished ...

Everyone looks for Rebecca, but she has left the scene ...

"There is no sign of her" says Josh

"Except" advises Josh

"Except what?" asks the responder

"Two white feathers" advises Josh

"White feathers?" asks the responder

"I told you she was an angel" insists Melanie

"How do you know?" asks the responder

"When white feathers appear ... angels are near" says Melanie

Number 6, Park Square East, Leeds city centre. Prestigious Barrister offices, a high-quality working environment ...

Angel's Eyes Investigations, Second floor suite, approx. 10.20am

Rebecca arrives late from the station ...

Rebecca is very striking, has long brown hair and piercing blue eyes ...

"Sorry I am late but there was panic at the station" advises Rebecca

"Yes, I know" advises Mary

Kate leaves the room ...

"They are saying that an angel healed a woman there" advises Mary

"Yes, they are right ... I healed her" advises Rebecca

"People saw you in broad daylight?" asks Mary

"She needed urgent attention ... besides no one saw me leave" insists Rebecca

"... but they might have caught your image on CCTV" advises Mary

"I doubt that Mary ... we are undetectable" insists Rebecca

"One day Rebecca ... you will get us all into trouble" says Mary

"Don't worry Mary, remember what Michael told us" advises Rebecca

"I remember ... no one on Earth can see who we really are" says Mary

"That's right ... our identities remain intact" says Rebecca

Kate returns to the office with the coffee's ...

Kate is in her mid-twenties and has long dark hair and green eyes ...

"Have I missed anything?" asks Kate

"Not really ... only Rebecca's encounter at the Railway station" advises Mary

"What encounter ... tell me all about it, Rebecca" asks Kate

"Tell her later Rebecca ... have you got the files Kate?" asks Mary

Kate brings over the case files to Rebecca and Mary ...

"We can now start our meeting" says Rebecca

"What do we have on the agenda today?" asks Mary

"We have a very delicate case to investigate" advises Kate

"Do we need to be on our guard Kate?" asks Rebecca

"Maybe, it concerns a fake fortune teller" advises Kate

"What?" asks Mary

"A clairvoyant ... a spiritualist" says Kate

"Really?" asks Rebecca

"Well, it has been reported that this lady called Samantha is a fraud ... yet no such evidence has ever been found" advises Kate

"Well, how can she be condemned as a fraud?" asks Mary

"They think that Samantha is taking money under false pretences and that is the fraud" advises Kate

"We must investigate this lady" advises Rebecca

"We've been asked to go under cover as clients?" advises Kate

"Under cover?" asks Mary

"It's just a term given to investigations, Mary" advises Rebecca

"Under cover … now I understand" laughs Mary

"Who has asked for the investigation to be carried out?" asks Rebecca

"Sorry, there doesn't seem to be a name on file" advises Kate

"OK … what's the address … we will go and investigate today" says Rebecca

"Why don't you accompany us, Kate?" asks Mary

"I would love to … I will arrange for a taxi" replies Kate

Within minutes a black and white cab arrives …

"Who has asked us to go under cover Kate?" asks Rebecca

"I will check the file again" advises Kate

Kate leaves the room …

"Don't you think that was a little unwise Mary asking Kate to accompany us?"

"She is a bright girl … I think we may benefit from her expertise" advises Mary

Kate returns with the file …

"The file says …" says Kate

"Yes" asks Rebecca

"It is a request from the Bishop of Leeds" advises Kate

"It must be very important" says Mary

"Let's not disappoint him then" advises Rebecca

Meanwhile, back at the Bar Convent in York … John Paul, Nicola, and Peter have equally been given a precarious investigation at the York Dungeon concerning ghostly apparitions …

Meeting Room One … Monday 11am …

"We will have to be on our guard today" advises John Paul

"Why?" asks Nicola

"This investigation concerns ghostly sightings at the York Dungeon" says John Paul

Peter checks the file …

"We have been asked to investigate by the owners" advises Peter

"What's the story Peter?" asks John Paul

"The York Dungeon is a museum, and it is open to the public … it specialises in York's history" advises Peter

"So, it's a tourist attraction?" asks Nicola

"Well, yes I suppose it is" advises Peter

"It also has special effects, displays of models and certain other objects" advises Peter

"Everything takes you back to the city's darkest age" advises Peter

"Your quite knowledgeable on this Peter" says Nicola

"Well, I used to work there a few years ago" advises Peter

"Now, we understand" says John Paul

"There's also another problem" advises Peter

"I suppose this will be about the apparitions?" says John Paul

"Indeed, it is … the owners say that ghostly spirits of Roman soldiers have started to appear" advises Peter

"Roman soldiers?" asks Nicola

"Have they started to rustle their chains?" asks John Paul

"Worse than that … they have started to disturb the ambience of the museum and began frightening people to death" advises Peter

"Frightening people to death … what a statement Peter" says Nicola

"You know what I mean … as in frightened out of their wits" advises Peter

"Now, we understand Peter" says Nicola

"OK contact the owners Peter ... tell them we will take up their case and investigate, but that we are not promising anything" advises John Paul

"Ask when we can commence our investigation" asks Nicola

Peter leaves the room and contacts the owners of the York Dungeon to set a time and date for the investigation to begin ...

"What do you think John Paul?" asks Nicola

"It is obvious that a solution needs to be found" advises John Paul

"We may need to use all our skills and intuition with regards this phenomenon" insists John Paul

"I agree ... it won't be easy" says Nicola

"It may take more than intuition to eradicate the museum of this problem" advises John Paul

"If it is a ghostly phenomenon we may have to tread carefully" adds Nicola

"Yes, I totally agree" advises John Paul

Back in Leeds, Rebecca, Mary, and Kate head out to see Samantha, who lives across the city to see what all the fuss is about ...

The black and white taxi drops them off outside of a semidetached house ...

Kate knocks on the door ...

They are all taken by surprise when a lady in a gypsy costume answers the door ...

"Hello, I am Samantha, please do not be alarmed the costume is all part of the make-up, clients find it appropriate and soothing ... how may I help you?" asks the voice

"I'm Rebecca, this is Mary and Kate"

"You rang for a reading?" asks Samantha

"Yes, I booked the reading" advises Kate

"Do you want a single or group reading?" asks Samantha

"What do you suggest?" asks Mary

"You can have a full reading or a simple reading" advises Samantha

"What's the cost of the readings?" asks Kate

"The full reading is £40, and it lasts an hour. A simple one costs £15, and it lasts for half an hour" advises Samantha

"We'll have the full reading please" says Rebecca

"Do you recommend that?" asks Mary

"Yes, indeed I do if it's a full reading" advises Samantha

"What's next?" asks Kate

"If you could all sit around the table, please" asks Samantha

"What do you intend to do first?" asks Rebecca

"I think a tarot reading first would be appropriate" advises Samantha

Samantha shuffles the tarot cards three times ... then splits them into three piles and takes the top card off each pile ...

"I can sense that you're not from Leeds and that you have a purpose in life" advises Samantha

"Purpose?" asks Mary

"I am from Leeds" advises Kate

"Yes, I believe you are, but your friends are not" advises Samantha

"What do your cards says about us?" asks Rebecca

"You possess a great gift from a great teacher ... and one not of this World" advises Samantha

"What else do your cards reveal?" asks Rebecca

"You seem to have great power at your disposal" adds Samantha

"Great power ... what does she mean?" asks Kate

"Samantha speaks the truth Kate" says Mary

"Please tell me ... who are you?" asks Samantha

"We are travellers from ... well, a long way from here" advises Mary

"You could say we specialise in helping people one way or another" advises Rebecca

Samantha turns to Kate and asks a question ...

"... and what is your role in all of this?" asks Samantha

"I work with Rebecca and Mary as a business associate" replies Kate

"You have links with the other side ... and you are both of significant importance" advises Samantha

"Significant importance ... I don't understand?" says Kate

"What Samantha is saying is that Mary and I have purpose in life and death" advises Rebecca

"What does that mean?" asks Kate

"You are not of this World, are you?" asks Samantha

"What is she saying Rebecca?" asks Kate

"We are from another time ... another place" advises Rebecca

"A bright light radiates from both of you" insists Samantha

"What about me?" asks Kate

"You're like me ... human" advises Samantha

"... and what do you make of us?" asks Rebecca

"My intuition tells me that your both angels" replies Samantha

"Your intuition is right ... we are both angels ... real angels and we are on God's mission to help and protect all living souls in this World" advises Rebecca

"You are both in great danger" advises Samantha anxiously

"Danger from whom?" asks Mary

"Not from whom ... but from what" advises Samantha

"I think we know of whom you speak" advises Rebecca

"Another force is against you" insists Samantha

"Who?" asks Mary

"A dark force ... who also has a purpose to destroy other's lives" advises Samantha

"Oh, we know all about him ... he doesn't stand a chance with the truth" advises Mary

"Why are you really here?" asks Samantha

"Someone has alledged that you are a fraud, but I can find no proof of that" advises Rebecca

"We ask only one thing of you Samantha" asks Mary

"What is that?" asks Samantha

"All we ask is for you to keep our secret ... you too Kate" says Rebecca

"Now we will give you our blessing by the touching of hands" says Rebecca

All four touch hands in a circle ...

"What happened?" asks Samantha

"I can't remember" says Kate

"There is no case here to answer Samantha. We believe in what you are doing. We can help each other again" advises Rebecca

"Has someone made a claim against me?" asks Samantha

"Yes, but it is completely unfounded" advises Mary

"We believe in you Samantha" advises Rebecca

"Thank you, I hope our paths cross again" adds Samantha

"I am sure they will" advises Mary

Rebecca, Mary, and Kate leave Samantha's house and return by taxi to Leeds ...

"You know it's funny" says Kate

"What is?" asks Mary

"I just can't remember anything about Samantha" advises Kate

"Isn't that strange?" says Kate

"Isn't it?" advises Rebecca

Back in York, at the Dungeon Museum, John Paul, Nicola, and Peter encounter all sorts of trickery ...

"It's just the tricks of the trade ... all part of the museum's invention and curiosity for the tourists" advises an assistant

"What about the Legion of Roman soldiers marching and chanting? asks John Paul

"Well, I know of the rumour ... but I have never seen them" advises Peter

"You may be about to witness them now" says John Paul

"Call them out" advises Nicola

John Pul shouts in a loud voice ...

"To all those in the benevolence of Caesar I command you to come forth"

There is no response to this command ... then suddenly, marching, which grows nearer with the arrival of a legion of Roman soldiers in a ghostly mist ...

Chariots and Horses with standard bearers and a full cohort of men ...

The Centurian in charge responds to John Paul's command ...

"On who's authority have you asked for our presence?" asks the Centurian

"On God's authority" replies John Paul

"I care not for you or your God" replies the Centurian

"Why are you marching?" asks Nicola

"To serve our Empire ... and to save York" replies the Centurian

"But don't you know ... we are over two thousand years in the *future" advises Nicola*

"And what year is it, may I ask" replies the Centurian

"2023" advises John Paul

"We are in 12AD ... our Emperor lives, and we are the toast of Rome" advises the Centurian

"You have no Emperor now" advises John Paul

"We have no God but Caesar" replies the Centurian

"Caesar asks you to stop and obey my authority" asks John Paul

"We don't recognise you or your authority" replies the Centurian

"This is going to be trickier than I thought ... have you any suggestions Nicola?" asks John Paul

"What about Caesar's wife Cornelia ... they may obey her command?" advises Nicola

"Do you think it will work?" asks John Paul

"We can try" advises Nicola

"I agree Nicola ... you assume the role of Cornelia" says John Paul

The Centurian stands firm, and the ghostly soldiers all stand to attention as if waiting for more orders ...

Nicola calls out to the Centurian ...

"Centurian ... I am Cornelia ... wife of Julius Caesar" advises Nicola

There is no response from the Centurian ...

"You know that I am above suspicion and as Caesar's wife I hold power of the Roman Empire?" advises Nicola

"Do you understand Centurian?" asks Nicola

"I understand" replies the Centurian

"I have been asked by Caesar to guide you to safety" advises Nicola

"Safety?" queries the Centurian

Peter now intervenes ...

"Would it be prudent if I helped in this matter?" asks Peter

"How?" asks Nicola

"What if I were to help by being a Roman Commander … surely the Centurian would then obey orders?" asks Peter

"Yes, I agree Peter … it might just work" advises John Paul

"Assume the role of Emperor Septimus Severus … he was well known to everyone in York" advises John Paul

"OK John Paul, I'll try!" says Peter

Peter calls out to the Centurian asking him to obey his commands …

"Centurian" asks Peter

The Centurian does not respond to his command …

"Centurian … I am Emperor Septimus Severus" advises Peter

"Emperor?" responds the Centurian

"Your journey to Eboracum is at an end … you must report to the Roman garrison where you and your men will find solace and rest" asks Peter

The Centurian stands rigid …

"Why do you not obey the command of your Emperor?" asks Peter

"My Emperor?" responds the Centurian

"Report to the Western Gate of the Roman fortress" asks Peter

"I will Inform the Praetorian Guards to guide you there" advises Peter

"Do you understand Centurian?" asks Peter

"Understood" replies the ghostly Centurian

The Praetorian Guard (Latin cohortes praetoria) were an elite unit of the Imperial Roman army that served as personal bodyguards and Intelligence agents for the Emperors.

During the Roman republic, the Praetorian Guards were an escort for high ranking officials, senators, and procurators and for senior officers of the Roman Legion.

The Centurian gives the command and begins to go forwards ...

"We will report as you command to the Western Gate of the Fortress" advises the Centurian

They disappear in a mist and go through a wall ...

"Well done, Peter" advises Nicola

"Yes, very well done ... you helped out in a very tricky situation" advises John Paul

"I don't think we could have done it without you, Peter" says John Paul

"Tell no one of what you have witnessed today, Peter" says Nicola

John Paul shakes Peter's hand ...

With that handshake Peter's memory of the meeting with the Centurian and the ghostly apparitions were erased ...

"Our work is done here" advises John Paul

"It's time for us to return to the Bar Convent" says Nicola

"What exactly happened here?" asks Peter

"Don't you remember Peter?" asks Nicola

"Sorry I can't remember anything" says Peter

"Fear not Peter ... the situation has been dealt with" advises John Paul

John Paul, Nicola, and Peter return to the entrance of the museum advising the owners that they have taken care of the ghostly apparitions and that they are now free of the phenomenon.

SUSPICIONS ... A MIRACLE IN LEEDS

Meanwhile, back in Leeds, Rebecca, Mary, and Kate deal with a visit involving a Monsignor from St. Anne's Cathedral ...

Inside Number 6, Park Square East, Leeds City Centre ... 2nd Floor suite ...

The bell rings outside the Angel's Eyes Investigations office ...

"Good afternoon, may I help you?" asks Kate

"Good afternoon ... I am Monsignor O'Brien ... I am from St Annes Cathedral"

"From the Cathedral?" asks Kate

"Yes, exactly ... I am here on official business" advises the Monsignor

Rebecca and Mary enter the offices ...

"May I present His Excellency the Monsignor from St Annes Cathedral?" advises Kate

"I am just a humble Monsignor" advises the priest

"Good afternoon Monsignor, ... I am Rebecca and this is Mary ... you have already met Kate" says Rebecca

"Charmed to meet you all" advises the Monsignor

"How can we help you?" asks Rebecca

"Is this an official visit, Monsignor?" asks Kate

"Yes, I am investigating into recent events ... with instructions from the Bishop" advises the Monsignor

"So how can we help you?" asks Mary

"What recent events?" asks Rebecca

"Please call me Brendan" advises the Monsignor

"How can we help you, Brendan?" asks Rebecca

"A young woman was recently healed at Leeds City Station" advises the Monsignor

"Healed?" asks Mary

"Yes ... she claims while she was waiting for the ambulance responder a woman healed her" advises the Monsignor

"A woman?" asks Rebecca

"As you can see ... we are all women here" says Kate

"We don't understand what has all this to do with us?" asks Mary

"Perhaps nothing ... perhaps everything!" says the Monsignor

"You call your agency Angel's Eyes Investigations, don't you?" asks the Monsignor

"Yes, but we don't have heavenly powers ... if that's what you mean?" says Kate

"If we had we would not be able to hide them ..., would we?" advises Rebecca

"As you can see for yourself ... we don't have any wings" says Mary

"As I see ... but whoever they are ... they could be in disguise" advises the Monsignor

"We're sorry that we can't help you any further, Monsignor" says Rebecca

"Thank you for your time … It was wonderful to meet you all" says the Monsignor

"Wonderful to meet you Monsignor, I mean Brendan. Thank you for calling" says Rebecca

"May God keep you in His prayers" advises the Monsignor

Kate escorts the Monsignor from the 2nd floor suite into Park Square …

Mary and Rebecca are left deep in conversation …

"Do you think he suspects?" asks Mary'

"Maybe, but he doesn't have any evidence, only a witness account" advises Rebecca

"We will all have to be on our guard in future" says Mary

"We may have to cloak ourselves in disguise" advises Rebecca

"To protect our true identities?" asks Mary

"Exactly" says Rebecca

Kate returns to the office …

"Well, I think we handled that pretty well" advises Kate

"Do you think we are under suspicion Kate?" asks Rebecca

"We may have to watch our step from now on" says Mary

"I think he is a nice man and doesn't mean any harm" advises Kate

The Monsignor returns to the Bishop's House at St Anne's Cathedral and directly reports his findings …

The Monsignor knocks on the door of the Bishop's quarters …

"Come in" says a voice

"Thank you, Eminence" says the Monsignor

"Monsignor O'Brien … did you investigate as requested?" asks the Bishop

"I did Eminence … I visited the Angel's Eyes Investigations offices as

you instructed" advises the Monsignor

"What did you find out?" asks the Bishop

"There is one thing in common ... it is an all-ladies office" advises the Monsignor

"Did you put your questions to them, Monsignor?" asks the Bishop

"Yes, I did at length, Eminence" advises the Monsignor

"Did they provoke a reaction?" asks the Bishop

"Several, Eminence" advises the Monsignor

"Have you come to any conclusions with their answers?" asks the Bishop

"I think they are hiding something" says the Monsignor

"Do you think they may have had something to do with the event at Leeds City Station, Monsignor?" asks the Bishop

"I think we may have to monitor them to find out the real truth" advises the Monsignor

"Very well, Monsignor, continue your investigations and advise me of anything else when known" advises the Bishop

"I will Eminence" assures the Monsignor

"If you require any help or assistance let me know" advises the Bishop

"Why all the cloak and dagger, Eminence?" asks the Monsignor

"News of what has happened has reached Rome, Brendan" advises the Bishop

"Rome?" asks the Monsignor

"It's no longer a local issue" advises the Bishop

"A meeting of the Cardinal's conclave has requested further information and we must advise whether something really took place" advises the Bishop

"Here in Leeds?" asks the Monsignor

"Yes, we must find out ... the ramifications could cause a multitude of claims" advises the Bishop

"I understand what you are saying Eminence" says the Monsignor

As the Monsignor leaves the meeting with the Bishop, a parishioner greets him with news from the Cathedral concerning a bleeding statue?

"There's been another development, this time in the Cathedral" advises Father Andrew

"What's happened?" asks the Monsignor

"It might be easier if you come and see for yourself" replies Father Andrew

Both the Monsignor and Father Andrew make their way into the Cathedral ...

Once inside the Cathedral they become surrounded by several parishioners looking and wanting answers ...

"We were just saying a decade of the rosary ... when suddenly" says Mrs McCabe

"Well go on woman ... what happened?" asks the Monsignor

"The statue of Our Lady ... started to bleed" advises the parishioner

"My God" says the Monsignor

"I will take a look at the statue, Brendan" advises Father Andrew

Father Andrew is away for several minutes, then returns and notifies the Monsignor ...

"Father Andrew did you find anything?" asks the Monsignor

"It was just a rusty pipe, Brendan" advises Father Andrew

"Yes, but did God cause the rusty pipe to happen?" asks the Monsignor

"I see ... as in an act of God?" says Father Andrew

"Yes, that very well could be the answer" says the Monsignor

"We should advise all the parishioners" says Father Andrew

"Why?" asks the Monsignor

"It's our duty" answers Father Andrew

"I will notify the Bishop … but we will leave things as they are Father Andrew"

"As they are?" asks Father Andrew

"Just imagine it Andrew … if we were to tell them the truth and the press got hold of it … they would have a field day" says the Monsignor

"We would leave ourselves wide open" advises the Monsignor

"I suppose your right Brendan" advises Father Andrew

"Believe me Andrew … I am right" says the Monsignor

"If the press did get hold of it … that would be at our expense" advises the Monsignor

"I understand now" says Father Andrew

Back at Number 6, Park Square, Rebecca, and Mary are chatting in the 2nd floor suite …

"I have just heard on Radio Leeds that something happened at the Cathedral this morning" advises Kate

"What are they saying Kate?" asks Rebecca

"Well, they are saying a miracle happened there today" advises Kate

"A miracle?" asks Rebecca

"The reporter says that a statue of Our Lady was said to be bleeding" advises Kate

"Really?" asks Mary

"Yes, really" advises Kate

Kate leaves the room to make a brew …

"Weren't you at the Cathedral this morning Mary?" asks Rebecca

"I don't suppose this has anything to with you, has it?" asks Mary

"Well?" asks Rebecca

"Well, was it to do with you Mary or not?" asks Rebecca

"I may have had something to do with it" replies Mary

"What did Michael say?" asks Rebecca

"Not to get involved" replies Mary

"I only wanted them to believe ... I think they needed it" advises Mary

"Mary, don't presume to believe ... our job is guiding lost souls" advises Rebecca

"That's what I was doing ... guiding" responds Mary

"The whole mission could now be in jeopardy" advises Rebecca

"I only wanted to help" says Mary

"We'll have to lie low for a while" advises Rebecca

"What if duty calls?" asks Mary

"We will have to change identity to protect who we really are" says Rebecca

"I understand ... I am sorry Rebecca" says Mary

"Honestly Mary, you still have a lot to learn" advises Rebecca

"Remember in future Mary, to be discreet" advises Rebecca

"I promise I will" says Mary

Kate returns from the kitchen with the coffee's ...

"Did I miss anything?" asks Kate

"We were just discussing business etiquette and procedure" says Rebecca

"Rebecca was putting me straight on several matters" advises Mary

"Is there anything I can help with?" asks Kate

"We're all done here" says Rebecca

"Now ... to the meeting" says Kate

Meanwhile, across the city, the Yorkshire Evening Post have been made aware of the recent occurrence at the Cathedral ...

"I've been checking ... there's a story coming out of St Anne's Cathedral" advises the reporter

"What's it all about?" asks the Editor

"They are saying that a statue was bleeding" advises the reporter

"It sounds unbelievable" advises the Editor

"Well, that's the story Boss" advises the reporter

"A statue, actually bleeding?" responds the Editor in disbelief

"OK, check with our sister paper in York ... haven't they reported something similar?" asks the Editor

"They were reporting about ghostly Roman soldiers marching and chanting, then disappearing through walls at the York Dungeon" replies the reporter

"I wonder ... both stories sound similar yet unsimilar" advises the Editor

"OK see what else you can find ... start digging" advises the Editor

"What about the Roman soldiers story?" asks the Editor

"I believe there was some controversy" advises the Editor

"That's right, you are correct" says the reporter

"Check and cross check to see if they are somehow linked" advises the Editor

"I'll get on to it straight away" advises the reporter

Meanwhile back at the Bar Convent in York, John Paul is looking into a problem concerning the Minster ...

"We have been asked to investigate concerning a sighting at the Minster" advises John Paul

"What's going on?" asks Nicola

"It would appear apparitions are causing mayhem in the crypt"
advises John Paul

"Apparitions?" asks Nicola

"Yes, recent excavations have unearthed certain religious artefacts causing disturbance with ancient burial chambers" advises John Paul

"How can we help?" asks Nicola

"I will talk to Peter and ask for his comments" advises John Paul

"Be careful John Paul, I think Peter is beginning to suspect something" warns Nicola

"You do know that he is in love with you, Nicola, don't you?" asks John Paul

"I did suspect something like that ... what am I going to do?" asks Nicola

"Don't do anything Nicola ... Peter won't harm our mission" advises John Paul

"If we need to, we will erase his memory of events" advises John Paul

"I will try and let him down easy" advises Nicola

Peter arrives at the Bar Convent and meets Nicola in the foyer ...

Peter blushes ...

"Nicola" says Peter

"Hello Peter ... have you heard of any problems at the Minster lately?" asks Nicola

"The Minster?" asks Peter

"Well, it may be only hear say but I have heard there has been talk of apparitions" advises Peter

"... hear say?" asks Nicola

"What I have heard on the grapevine" explains Peter

"You heard things ... on the grapevine?" says Nicola

"A bit like Marvin Gaye … he heard it through the grapevine" says Peter

"Marvin Gaye?" asks Nicola

"Oh, I will tell you about him sometime … over a beer" advises Peter

"Is that what you call a date Peter?" asks Nicola

"If you wish, Nicola" advises Peter

John Paul enters asking Nicola if Peter has spoken about the Minster …

"Well, he says he heard it through the grapevine?" advises Nicola

"Is Peter talking in code?" asks Nicola

"A Marvin Gaye fan … so, am I?" advises John Paul

"Who is Marvin Gaye?" asks Nicola

"I was just explaining to Nicola" advises Peter

"Maybe we can listen to Marvin together, Peter?" asks Nicola

"I'm sure that can be arranged love" replies Peter

"I will look forward to it" responds Nicola

John Paul and Nicola go into another room at the Bar Convent …

"If you could please get the coffees Peter, we will be in the meeting room" advises John Paul

Peter leaves for the kitchen …

"We need to find out what is happening at the Minster, John Paul" advises Nicola

"I thought you were going to let Peter down gently?" asks John Paul

"Sorry, I couldn't do it" advises Nicola

"You were flirting with Peter" says John Paul

"Flirting?" asks Nicola

"Yes, by saying you will arrange to be with him to listen to Marvin Gaye" advises John Paul

"Don't worry John Paul … it's all very innocent" advises Nicola

"You must remember … we cannot love human beings here on earth" advises John Paul

"Yes, I know … we are spiritual beings" responds Nicola

"Yes exactly, why can't you remember that?" asks John Paul

"I can still remember and feel my human side" advises Nicola

"I know how you feel Nicola, we were also once human … but we are now angels, and we are here on Earth for a purpose" advises John Paul

"Please try Nicola, to be careful, and keep your emotions under control" advises John Paul

"I promise I will try John Paul, but it won't be easy" advises Nicola

"The longer it goes on the harder it will become" says John Paul

"Don't worry, I know what I am doing" says Nicola

THE TORCHLIGHT PROCESSION

Meanwhile, back at number 6 Park Square in Leeds city centre, Mary, Rebecca, and Kate decide to attend the Torchlight Procession in Batley …

Kate enters the meeting room with several files ...

"I have been looking at the local Catholic paper and seen that a Torchlight Procession is being held tonight" advises Kate

"Is it far?" asks Rebecca

"No ... just a few miles from here in Batley" advises Kate

"Is this the first time it has taken place?" asks Mary

"No, according to what is written in the paper it has been taking place annually since 1951" advises Kate

"Since 1951 ... that's amazing" says Rebecca

"We must go there Rebecca, to witness such devotion" says Mary

"I agree, Mary" advises Rebecca

"We will all go together ... I am really looking forward to it" says Kate

It is now 6pm and Mary, Rebecca, and Kate begin their journey to Batley.

When they arrive in Batley Market Place, they are greeted by a Marshal who asks them not to park in the square...

"Sorry Miss ... you can't park here ... if you could park next to the Nash" advises the Marshal

"The Nash?" asks Mary

"Sorry we're from Leeds ... where exactly is the Nash?" asks Rebecca

"It's just over there, love" advises the Marshal

"Ah yes I see it now ... the Nash" replies Rebecca

"Why did he call you love ... does he mean he loves you?" asks Mary

"No Mary, it is just an expression here ... like please and thank you" says Kate

"I like their way of saying please and thank you" says Rebecca

"So do I" responds Mary

The car is parked safely then all three return on foot to the Market Place …

"Did you manage to park?" asks the Marshal

"Yes, thank you love" says Mary

Rebecca and Kate look in astonishment …

"Mary?" asks Rebecca

"I was only saying please and thank you" advises Mary

"I think you made his day" says Kate

It is now 7.30pm and the Market Place is full of people who then walk in a torchlight procession up to St Mary's Church in Cross bank …

The Parish Priest gives a homily on the Town Hall steps then announces over a microphone …

"I would like to welcome you all to Batley and to our annual Torchlight procession" advises Father John

"May I present the dignitaries" advises Father John

After a token homily the priest asks everyone to follow behind in procession for the mile walk to St Mary's RC Church.

Local news reporters from the Batley News are in attendance and are taking photographs to mark the event …

"It's amazing" advises Rebecca

"What is amazing?" asks Kate

"I have only witnessed this before in Lourdes" advises Rebecca

"So have I" says Mary

"I thought you would both like it" says Kate

"We do … it's just a pity Nicola and John Paul are not here" says Rebecca

Suddenly someone in the crowd shouts for help …

"Please will someone help me; my friend is having a seizure" says a voice

A woman in the crowd is in distress …

"We must help … before it's too late" says Mary

"We're out in the open here Mary … everyone will see" advises Rebecca

"Isn't that the reason why we are here?" says Mary

"So that we can be seen and not hiding from the truth?" says Mary

"I agree Mary … let's see how we can help" says Rebecca

"I am desperate, please help me" says a lady in the crowd

"We have come to help" advises Mary

"Let my friend help you" says Mary

"OK … how can we help you?" asks Rebecca

"What's the ladies name?" asks Mary

"Veronica … she is called Veronica" advises her friend

Rebecca kneels beside Veronica and starts to massage her chest …

"Can you hear me, Veronica?" asks Rebecca

There is no response …

Rebecca lays her hands on Veronica's chest and a glow begins to radiate … a brilliant white light …

"I'm here to heal you" advises Rebecca

"I will help you" advises Mary

The brilliant white light continues to intensify and draws a lot of attention …

"My God" says her friend

A crowd from the procession begin to gather round watching the dramatic scene unfolding before their eyes …

"Can you hear me now Veronica?" asks Rebecca

"If you can, sit up" asks Rebecca

Veronica astonishingly sits up unaided as instructed …

"I am alright … who are you?" asks Veronica

"You have saved me" says Veronica

"Your faith has saved you Veronica" advises Rebecca

"Thank you for saving Veronica … praise the Lord" says her friend

"We must leave now … our identities must be protected … tell no one" advises Rebecca

Kate rejoins Mary and Rebecca at the scene …

"My God … what happened here?" asks Kaye

"A miracle … it's a miracle" shouts a voice in the crowd

"We must leave now … follow me" advises Kate

"We will follow" says Rebecca

"Remember tell no one … keep our secret" advises Mary

As Kate, Mary and Rebecca leave the scene an ambulance responder arrives and pulls up in the marketplace followed by an emergency ambulance …

"Are you alright … what happened here?" asks the responder

"Two angels … they were two angels … they saved my life" advises Veronica

"Praise be to God" says a lady in the crowd

"What are you saying?" asks the responder

"It's a miracle, that lady was in a seizure and now she lives" say voices in the crowd

The Responder checks his equipment and checks Veronica's pulse and chest …

"I can find nothing wrong with this lady" advises the responder

"We told you … it's a miracle" say the crowd

"I'll call it in" advises the responder

"They'll never believe it" advises the responder

The Emergency Ambulance arrives on the scene in the Market Place and the responder puts them in the picture ...

News reporters from the Batley News arrive on the scene ...

"OK ... can anyone tell us what happened here?" asks a reporter

He is met by silence from the crowd ...

"Someone must have seen something ... we know something significant happened here tonight" says the reporter

No answer from anyone in the crowd ...

"We will get to the bottom of this, with or without your help" advises the reporter

Yet again no answer from the crowd ...

"Come on Charlie we won't get anything here" says the reporter

The news of Veronica's healing becomes the toast of the town. When the procession continues its journey to St Mary's there is lots of talk on the agenda.

Inside St Mary's RC Church ... it is full to the rafters with parishioners and others who have made the journey of faith from all over the Leeds diocese ...

"Please all be seated" advises Father John

"I have heard the news that angels may well have been present at the Torchlight in Batley tonight" continues Father John

"Wonderful things have happened ... Veronica who had a seizure in the Market Place has been healed" advises Father John

"We should take this as a sign from God" advises Father John

"He is watching over each and every one of us" advises Father John

Next day at the Batley News Offices ...

"Something really happened last night, Boss" says a reporter

"Have you checked the camera footage in the Market square?" asks the Editor

"No, not yet" advises the reporter

"Well, make that your first priority" instructs the Editor

"I will ask for approval from the Council and check back to you later" says the reporter

"Very well … I want to know what really happened last night" says the Editor

"Every minute detail no matter how small" says the Editor

"We understand" advises the reporter

EVERY CLOUD HAS A SILVER LINING

PARK SQUARE, 2ND FLOOR, ANGEL'S INVESTIGATIONS OFFICES … EARLY

Morning meeting … Kate, Rebecca and Mary are in attendance …

"Good morning, Kate … anything on the agenda today?" asks Rebecca

"Well, the press keep snooping" advises Kate

"Snooping?" asks Mary

"Checking … into everything" advises Kate

"I think we may have kept them at bay" says Rebecca

"One way or another" advises Mary

"So Kate, what have we today?" asks Rebecca

"There is a massive get together today in Roundhay Park … do you fancy going there?" asks Kate

"Mm ... that sounds nice ... perhaps we can have a day off" asks Mary

"Remember what Michael told us "advises Rebecca

"Oh, it will be fun ... won't it, Kate?" says Mary

"Well, a lot of things will be going off there that's for sure" advises Kate

"OK, you have convinced me ... perhaps we do need some stimulation" advises Rebecca

Meanwhile, back in York, John Paul, Nicola, and Peter encounter strange goings on in the streets ...

The centre of York is quite busy, bustling with tourists from all over the World and there are street entertainers on every corner ...

"Tell me Peter, what is all this busking about?" asks Nicola

"Oh, it's another modern-day phenomenon" advises Peter

"Phenomenon?" asks John Paul

"Well to me it all seems very strange, I can tell you" advises John Paul

"Then there's modern-day poverty on the street too" advises Peter

"That should not be happening now" advises Nicola

"You would be surprised how many people are on the breadline" says Peter

"Breadline?" puzzles Nicola

"Oh, it's just another word for poverty" advises Peter

"But this is a big City" says John Paul

"Every cloud has a silver lining" insists Peter

"Shall we visit the National Railway Museum?" asks Peter

"You will love it ... you must see the bullet train" insists Peter

"Bullet train ... is it fired out of a gun?" asks Nicola

"No, it transports people" advises Peter

"Now I am really confused" says Nicola

The National Railway Museum is on Leeman Road on the outskirts of the city.

You can explore the past, the present and the future of the railways there. It is also, home to many magnificent steam locomotives such as Mallard and the Flying Scotsman ... all of which are still working today ...

John Paul, Nicola, and Peter arrive on the concourse and are in awe of the massive beasts in the museum, but encounter problems along the way ...

"Help ... can anyone help me?" cries a woman

"How can we help?" asks John Paul

"Quick ... my husband has collapsed, and he is not breathing" says the woman

"Where's the defibrillator?" asks Peter

"Too far away to help me" advises the man gasping for breath

"I'll get help" advises Peter

"May we look at him and see if he is, OK?" asks Nicola

"We may have to act fast ... do we have your permission?" asks John Paul

"Please ... please do what you can" says the woman

"OK ... please stand back and give us some room" advises John Paul

"What is his name?" asks John Paul

"Oh, Roger ... my name is Beth" advises the woman

"Roger ... can you hear me?" asks John Paul

A bright light suddenly radiates from the laying of hands ...

"What's happening?" asks Roger

"Don't worry ... it's all part of the healing process" advises John Paul

"A new type of healing" says Nicola

After a few minutes Roger responds and is sitting upright …

"Are you alright, Roger?" asks Beth

"If it hadn't been for …" says Roger

"Been for whom love, there's no one here" advises Beth

Peter returns with the defibrillator to find no one at the scene …

Back in Leeds, Rebecca, Mary, and Kate are just arriving at the festival in Roundhay Park …

The crowd is enormous and there is live entertainment everywhere …

"It's such a big occasion" says Mary

"It reminds me of … well, a long time ago" advises Mary

"Long ago?" asks Kate

"Oh, she is a free spirit … Mary likes to reminisce" says Rebecca

After walking around the large lake and taking in the atmosphere of the fair a little girl falls out of a rowing boat and is in distress …

"Can someone help me … my little girl?" shouts a voice

Mary, Rebecca, and Kate run over to the distressed woman …

"What's her name?" asks Mary

"Rebecca" says the woman

"That's my name too" advises Rebecca

"Don't worry, we will save her" says Mary

"How?" asks the woman

The little girl is in shock by now and has been brought back on to dry land by others on the lake …

"Rebecca, can you hear me?" asks Mary

"Lay her down" says Mary

"My name is Mary … this is my friend, and she is also called Rebecca" says Mary

"Can you hear me, Rebecca?" asks Mary

"Stay with us, hold on, your now back on dry land" advises Mary

The young girl is hardly breathing …

"We're going to lay our hands on you … to save you" advises Rebecca

"Do we have your permission?" asks Rebecca

The young girl's mother nods … she is also in shock …

"You're a special little girl Rebecca … now breathe when I tell you" advises Mary

The little girl breathes as instructed, but falls into a coma …

"We're losing her" says Mary

The young girl's mother goes into hysterics …

"Rebecca … you will feel a power go through your body" says Mary

"Do exactly as I tell you" says Rebecca

"What's happening?" asks the young girl's mother

"We are your guardian angels Rebecca … you will live again … now do as I tell you" advises Mary

A crowd has now gathered round, and they are witnessing what is happening …

The little girl responds to the warm glow … and the bright lights.

Mary, Rebecca and Kate have suddenly all left the scene …

"It's a miracle" says Paula

"My little girl was almost dead … and now she lives" says Paula

"A miracle" shouts someone in the crowd

"How can I thank them?" asks Paula

"No one knows who they are" says another voice

"Look over there …" says a voice

A mound of white feathers on the ground …

"They saved my little girl's life" insists Paula

"They are gone, all that is left are ... white feathers"

"White feathers appear when angels are near" says Paula

Back at the press office at the Evening Post, reporters and Editors are having a field day ...

"Two miracles in one day ... one in Leeds and the other in York"

"We can't call them miracles" advises the Editor

"It's a kind of phenomenon ... with no explanation" insists the reporter

"If we report it as angel's ... well you know what everyone would think" advises the Editor

"Besides, we have no evidence at all to substantiate that claim, so we will have to stick to the unexplained for now" insists the Editor

"But it does clarify something" says the Editor

"What?" asks a reporter

"That two sets of people are operating in Leeds and in York" says the Editor

"So, tread carefully ... they are bound to make a mistake sometime" advises the Editor

Back in York at the Bar Convent, John Paul and Nicola are in a meeting ...

"We have managed to cover our tracks so far" advises John Paul

"No one suspects us" says Nicola

"Yes, our good deeds are now being praised all over the city" says John Paul

Peter walks into the meeting room ...

"You're both held in very high esteem" advises Peter

"Well, it's a natural phenomenon ... all we have to do is stick to the plan" says John Paul

"Michael will be pleased" advises Nicola

"Who is Michael?" asks Peter

"Our Boss" says John Paul

Peter starts to feel unwell …

"Are you alright Peter?" asks John Paul

Peter suffers a seizure …

"What's the matter Peter?" asks Nicola

There is no response from Peter …

"He's starting to turn blue" advises Nicola

"Quickly … let's lay our hands on him … do exactly as I say" advises John Paul

A radiance of dazzling light now beams from the angel's …

"It's going to take all our strength to save him" says John Paul

"Whatever happens, we must save Peter" says Nicola

The sheer dynamism and exposure to the light helps Peter to regain consciousness …

Peter starts to come round …

"What happened?" asks Peter

"We thought we had lost you?" advises John Paul

"Where's Nicola?" asks Peter

"What's happened to her?" asks Peter

"She needs to rest Peter" advises John Paul

"Why?" asks Peter

"You see we really are angels Peter, but our powers were almost drained saving you" advises John Paul

"Real angels?" asks Peter

"We both need to rest and communicate with Michael" says John Paul

"Michael?" asks Peter

"Yes, Michael … he is our Boss, and he is the Archangel" advises John Paul

"Do you mean Michael the Archangel?" asks Peter

"Yes … we were sent here by Michael" advises John Paul

"You really are both angels?" asks Peter

"Yes Peter … we really are" advises John Paul

"You need to keep our secret Peter" asks John Paul

"You saved my life John Paul … of course I will" says Peter

"You need to rest too Peter" insists John Paul

"What about Nicola?" asks Peter

"We will see how Nicola is later … and I will let you know" promises John Paul

"I love Nicola … John Paul" says Peter

"I know … we all love Nicola … you're a special man Peter" advises John Paul

"Tell Nicola, won't you?" says Peter

"Tell her what?" asks Nicola

"Oh, that I am so grateful" responds Peter

"I know Peter … and I love you too" says Nicola

"But we are not of this World … we all were once, and we are now in God's charge and angels watching over everyone" says Nicola

"So, there are more of you?" asks Peter

"More than you think in the World" advises John Paul

"Rebecca and Mary are also angels" says Nicola

"Promise to keep our secret and tell no one" says Nicola

"I promise I will" insists Peter

"To ensure that you do we have to touch you now to erase your memory of that we have said … all you will remember is being *saved" advises John Paul*

"What about you Nicola will I always remember you love me?" asks Peter

"For all eternity … for all eternity" advises Nicola

"Take me with you" asks Peter

"We can't Peter, you are still mortal … and you have your whole life in front of you" says Nicola

"We will meet again … to you it may seem a long time but to God it is only the blink of an eye" says Nicola

FAITHFUL TO THE END

Peter's recovery and mortality. The cross over. Nicola's confession. Mary Magdalene …

Early morning, Number 6 Park Square, Angel's Eyes Investigations, Leeds city centre …

"Your Mum is a caring soul Kate" advises Mary

"She helped everyone at the hospital, yet she didn't help herself" says Mary

"Who is Bernadette?" asks Rebecca

"Oh, she devoted her life to her family and all the patients at Leeds

General Infirmary … but she is dying now, and she is my Mum" advises Kate

"What is she dying of?" asks Mary

"Terminal cancer" advises Kate

"No one knows who … where or why it happened … it has come like a bolt out of the blue" says Kate

"Was she a friend of yours, Kate?" asks Rebecca

"She is very close … she is my Mum" advises Kate

"Oh, Kate we are so sorry … is there anything we can do?" asks Rebecca

"Maybe if you visit her in hospital, it might give her strength" asks Kate

"You see she has always , and she is a practising Catholic" advises Kate

"OK … take us there Kate … we'll see what we can do" advises Rebecca

Back in York, at the Bar Convent, Peter is making a speedy recovery …

"Your under doctor's orders now" insists Angelica

"Don't fuss woman … I am OK" says Peter

"Peter, it is for your own good" advises Nicola

"Mortality is such a frail thing … your prone to all types of wear and tear" advises Nicola

"Being mortal is only just part of it" advises John Paul

"Now rest, just like Angelica has asked you to do" asks John Paul

"I will watch over you" advises Nicola

"Oh, Nicola that would be wonderful" says Peter

John Paul asks Nicola several questions concerning Peter's welfare …

"Does he remember anything about what happened?" asks John Paul

"I doubt it ... I think that part of his memory has been erased" says Nicola

"Remember we are not of this World Nicola ... human love is still within reach, but we have a job to do" advises John Paul

"Don't worry John Paul, I know all about that" says Nicola

Back in Leeds, Rebecca, Mary, and Kate are on their way to Leeds General Infirmary to see Kate's mum ...

"Which ward is your Mum in?" asks Mary

"Ward 21" advises Kate

"We had better find it as soon as possible" says Rebecca

"We will follow our instincts" advises Mary

"Oh Mum" sighs Kate

They enter Ward 21 and find that all the curtains are drawn around Bernadette's bed. Doctors and nurses are quite busy rushing about ...

"How is she?" asks Kate

"Who are you?" asks a doctor

"Oh, she is my mum ... I am her ..." responds Kate

"She is her daughter, Kate" advises Mary

"And you are?" asks the doctor

"We are her friends and business partners" advises Rebecca

"What is happening?" asks Rebecca

"The chemo is not helping" advises the doctor

"... and it's spreading to the brain ... there is very little we can do" says the doctor

"Can we help?" asks Rebecca

"Maybe we can help?" says Mary

The Doctor leaves and attends to another patient ...

Mary and Rebecca decide to act ...

"If we can lay our hands on Bernadette it might help" says Rebecca

The Doctor returns …

"Do you agree to this Kate?" asks the doctor

"We specialise in helping people" advises Mary

"Please let them do as they ask … I trust them completely" advises Kate

"Very well" advises the doctor

Both Rebecca and Mary place their hands on Bernadette and a brilliant light starts to radiate …

"Bernadette, can you hear me?" asks Rebecca

"I hear you" replies Bernadette

"Why am I out of my body?" asks Bernadette

"It is almost time to go Bernadette" says Rebecca

"Who are you?" asks the doctor

"We are angels … Rebecca and Mary" says Rebecca

"We are here to help you cross over into the love of God" advises Mary

"Cross over … but I am afraid" says Bernadette

"Don't be afraid" says Mary

"God knows the heart" says Rebecca

"Where is my Kate?" asks Bernadette

"She is here at your bedside" says Rebecca

"Don't let her see me like this" asks Bernadette

"Tell her I am sorry for failing her as a Mum" says Bernadette

"No one fails in God's eyes" assures Mary

"Mum, you never failed me" insists Kate

"What's happening" asks Kate

There is an uneasy silence …

"Your Mum has passed to the other side" advises Rebecca

"She is now in God's hand, but she didn't suffer" advises Mary

"If only I could have done something" says Kate

"No one could help her" advises Mary

"We tried … but it was time for her to leave … her body was too frail to respond" says Rebecca

"We did our best Kate" says Mary

All three hug and there are many tears …

"Thank you for all you have done for my Mum" says Kate

"She is at peace now … remember you will meet her again" says Rebecca

"In Heaven?" asks Kate

"Yes, in Heaven … we all will" advises Mary

Rebecca touches Kate on the arm and also the doctor …

"What happened here?" asks the doctor

"I can't remember" insists Kate

Back in York at the Bar Convent, Angelica joins John Paul while Nicola stays to watch over Peter …

"Are you comfortable?" asks Nicola

"Yes, I am … thank you Nicola" says Peter

"You know there is something about you that I don't quite understand" says Peter

"Is there Peter … what do you mean?" asks Nicola

"I don't know what it is, but you are very caring and …" says Peter

"And what, Peter?" asks Nicola

"You do know that I am in love with you Nicola … don't you?" replies Peter

"Yes, I know Peter" says Nicola

"And ... it is a wonderful thing too" responds Nicola

"May I kiss you?" asks Peter

"Oh, sorry Peter, that is not possible" advises Nicola

"Why?" asks Peter

"I am an angel ... that's why" advises Nicola

"But I love you Nicola" says Peter

"I know you do but I am no longer mortal like you ... perhaps when you pass over?" says Nicola

Peter is in a state of delirium, but he continues to question Nicola ...

"Yes?" asks Peter

"I will be waiting for you" responds Nicola

"How long do I have to wait?" asks Peter

"For all Eternity" advises Nicola

"I was once human like you, and I had a different name" replies Nicola

"What was your name then?" asks Peter

"Magdolina" replies Nicola

"As in Mary of Magdaline?" asks Peter

"Possibly" replies Nicola

"You know who Mary was don't you Peter?" asks Nicola

"Yes, and what she was" says Peter

John Paul and Angelica return ...

"I know who you are" advises Peter

"What have you been saying Nicola?" asks John Paul

"Peter, we need you to be our contact on Earth" asks John Paul

"Contact?" asks Peter

"I know, but I love Nicola" advises Peter

"Of course, you do … Nicola is a kindred spirit" advises John Paul

"We are not of this World, Peter" responds John Paul

"We have been sent by God to watch over the World and to help those in distress" advises John Paul

"Do you understand?" asks Nicola

"Mortal love is forbidden" says John Paul

"Nicola loves me, John Paul" advises Peter

"Yes, I know she does but you will have to keep our secret, you too Angelica" insists John Paul

"How do we do that?" asks Peter

"We will touch you and your questions and memory will be erased. You will only remember the here and now and that you are working with us" advises John Paul

"Let it be done" advises Peter

"Remember I love you, Nicola" says Peter

"Remember I love you too, Peter" says Nicola

"For all Eternity" says Peter

John Paul and Nicola contact Peter and Angelica. Both their memories are erased of recent events …

"How long have I been asleep?" asks Peter

"A few hours" advises John Paul

"I had very strange dreams" replies Peter

"What do you remember?" asks Nicola

"Something about love and eternity … do you understand?" asks Peter

"Sorry Peter I don't but it may all have happened while you were dreaming" advises Nicola

"Strange … it all seemed very real" says Peter

TELEPHONE EXCHANGE
TO HEAVEN

The Angel's are questioned about self-doubting, eternal life and having a pure heart. A significant trauma takes place. Michael the Archangel intervenes. The Angel's encounter exorcism and a change of identity. Nicola agrees to help in a where and when situation ...

PARK SQUARE, LEEDS CITY CENTRE ... 2nd FLOOR, ANGEL'S EYES INVESTIGATIONS ... IN THE MEETING ROOM ...

"Did you ever have any doubts?" asks Kate

"Doubts?" replies Rebecca

"In whom you are ... why we are here ... where am I going ... you know ... doubts?" asks Kate

"No ... never" replies Rebecca

"We are both incapable of doubting" advises Mary

"You know the story of doubting Thomas, don't you?" replies

Rebecca

"Yes, I know it very well" responds Kate

"He needed to see the reality of everything before he could believe … all you need is faith to believe, Kate" says Rebecca

"I feel so lost now my Mum has gone" says Kate

"She may not be here in person, but she is still very much in your life" assures Mary

"How do you know Mary?" asks Kate

"Because we believe in the truth and Jesus is the way, the life and the truth" replies Mary

"… and through Him all things are possible. He has the message of Eternal Life … believe Kate in your faith and let us help you" advises Rebecca

"I will, thank you" assures Kate

"How can we show you how to believe more than you do?" asks Mary

"You can start by telling me who you really are and why you are here" asks Kate

Meanwhile, back in York, Nicola and John Paul continue to aid Peter in his recovery …

"If only I could have married you, Nicola" says Peter

"Married me … why?" asks Nicola

"You're so beautiful, so innocent and pure of heart" advises Peter

"You know why that is Peter, don't you?" responds Nicola

John Paul enters and pulls Nicola to one side …

"I thought we had erased everything" asks John Paul

"The heart sees and believes only what it wants to believe … the brain records and remembers significant traumas in life" advises Nicola

"Yet, we are not in life, Nicola" says John Paul

"I am always with you Peter ... think of me as your guardian angel" replies Nicola

"If only I could join you?" replies Peter

"I think he is remembering again" advises John Paul

"In time Peter you will ... but you have all your life ahead of you" says Nicola

"God will guard and protect in all that you do" informs Nicola

"Until the end of time?" asks Peter

"Yes, until the end of time and beyond ... there is no time when you pass into the afterlife" advises John Paul

"We call it ... Heaven" advises Nicola

"Yes, it has many names ... the hereafter ... the afterlife and so on" responds John Paul

"God is watching over all of us" advises Nicola

"Now sleep Peter ... you need to rest" asks John Paul

Back in Leeds, at Park Square, Rebecca and Mary join hands and a beam of light radiates from their bodies ...

"Watch Kate ... but say nothing" advises Rebecca

"What is happening?" asks Kate

"Good day Michael ... are you pleased with all that we are doing on Earth?" asks Rebecca

"I am well pleased with all of you" responds Michael

"Who is with you?" asks Michael

"Kate ... she has recently lost her Mum" advises Rebecca

"Tell Kate, she is now in God's Kingdom and has she got a message for her?" advises Michael

Kate is frightened at witnessing the apparition ... then finds the courage to speak ...

"Please ask my Mum for forgiveness ... and tell her that I am sorry we

could not save her" advises Kate

"No one could save your Mum … it was beyond human help … but she lives as a free spirit in God's Kingdom" advises Michael

"She wants to communicate with you" advises Michael

"I would be glad to talk to her" responds Kate

"Sit down Kate" asks Rebecca

Kate sits around the table with Mary and Rebecca …

"My darling Kate don't be sad at my passing" says a voice

"Is it you Mum?" asks Kate

"Yes … I am still with you, and I am still watching over you" responds the voice

"Don't fear about carrying on with your life" says the voice

"There is someone else who wants to talk to you" says the voice

"Hello Kate … it's your dad" responds another voice

"My dad?" asks Kate

"Listen to what your Mum says … we are reunited now … in time you will join us … enjoy your life" says the voice

"Is that really you dad?" asks Kate

"Yes, and I am here through the power of God … listen to what they have to say" says the voice

"Who?" asks Kate

"The angels who are with you now … believe in them" says the voice

"I will … God bless you Mum and Dad" says Kate

"God bless you too" responds the voice

The link to Heaven with Kate's Mum and Dad is broken …

"Thank you so much" says Kate

"Kate, you deserved to know the truth" advises Rebecca

"You see in reality we really are angels, all we ask is that you keep our

secret" asks Mary

"I promise I will" responds Kate

"To keep our promise, we need you to join hands with us" says Mary

"Why?" asks Kate

"We need to erase your thoughts, and to protect our true identities" responds Rebecca

"OK, I agree" advises Kate

Back in York at the Bar Covent, John Paul, Nicola, and Angelica are requested by Samantha … the spiritualist and clairvoyant, to help in a tricky situation …

"I would be grateful if you could assist me in an exorcism" asks Samantha

"We're not here to cast out spirits, but to help those in need" replies John Paul

"What seems to be the problem?" asks Nicola

"A demon at the York Castle" advises Samantha

"A demon?" asks John Paul

"Really, in modern day York?" replies Nicola

"What exactly is happening?" asks John Paul

"Chains are being rattled and there are lots of weird noises" advises Samantha

"Are you sure it's not one of Yorks modern day effects?" asks John Paul

"I am reliably informed, that it is not" replies Samantha

"What exactly do you want us to do?" asks John Paul

"If you could assist Father McGuire in everything?" asks Samantha

"OK, we will do it" advises John Paul

"We will allow it on this occasion" replies Nicola

"But, we don't specialise in casting out spirits" advises John Paul

York Castle museum is close to Clifford's Tower in the centre of York ...

John Paul, Nicola, and Samantha arrange to meet Father McGuire as requested near the entrance to the museum ...

Father McGuire is in his early sixties, he has silver hair and dressed in an all black suit ...

"Thank you for joining me" advises Father McGuire

"I am John Paul, this is Nicola, and you already know Samantha" advises John Paul

"Now, how can we assist you, Father?" asks John Paul

"I will carry out the exorcism ... but if you can be on hand?" asks Father McGuire

"We can watch over you if that is what you want?" advises Nicola

"Are you sure it's a real phenomenon Father?" asks John Paul

"It could be a prankster" responds Samantha

"A prankster?" asks John Paul

"Oh, someone taking the mickey" advises Samantha

"Taking the mickey?" asks Nicola

"Well, taking the Michael then" advises Samantha

"Better not tell Michael about any of this, especially the bit about taking the mickey" replies Nicola

"Michael ... Michael who?" asks Father McGuire

"Oh, just someone we know" advises John Paul

"Well, don't worry your secret is safe with us" says Father McGuire

"No need for nerves" advises Father McGuire

"Call out the demon" asks John Paul

The Priest starts to recite some words in Latin asking the spirit to show themselves ...

"Come forth" asks Father McGuire

There is no response to his requests …

The Priest asks a second time …

At the second command two children appear in ghostly costumes with sound effects …

"It's all been a hoax" advises Samantha

"Sorry … we didn't mean any harm, lady" says a young boy

"Well, it is nearly Halloween" resonds the Priest

"No harm done" says Nicola

"The real harm is those children dressing up and meddling in the occult" advises John Paul

"It's just a bit of fun" says a young boy

"There is no fun in playing Satan" advises Nicola

"OK … we are both sorry … we won't do it again" say the boys

Meanwhile, back at Angel's Eyes Investigations in Park Square, Rebecca, Mary, and Kate are looking at yet another case …

Local Sex Workers are caught up in major problems with the Police …

"We may have to ask Nicola to intervene on this one" advises Rebecca

"Why?" asks Mary

"When she was human, she had a different name … Magdolina" advises Rebecca

"As in Mary of Magdelin?" asks Mary

"Yes … the very same" answers Rebecca

"You remember who Mary was don't you?" asks Rebecca

"Yes, I remember" replies Mary

"But isn't she Mary of Bethany and related to Lazarus?" asks Mary

"Yes, I believe she is" says Rebecca

"Still Nicola will be perfect for this case" advises Rebecca

"She may have to change her identity to do so" replies Mary

"Oh, I think Magdolina ... I mean Nicola will relish the job in hand" advises Rebecca

"OK ... we will get her on the case" says Rebecca

Rebecca and Mary talk to Nicola and make her aware of the problem ...

"I will be glad to help ... of course I will assume my role again in a modern way" advises Nicola

"Tell me where and when and I will be there" says Nicola

ABDUCTION AND REDEMPTION

PART ONE – ABDUCTED

When a young woman is abducted in York, after spending a night in the city centre with her friends, problems arise for the angels.

John Paul is recognised at the scene of the abduction.

The Police are unable to locate the missing young woman's whereabouts.

The Angel's Eyes Agency help the Police to trap the abductor and free John Paul as well as keeping his identity a secret.

Meanwhile in Leeds, Rebecca, Mary, and Kate attend a Singles Dance in the city centre and as per usual it is a night of more than just dancing!

As they leave the venue with Peter and Kate, they notice an overturned car and help to rescue and free the occupants.

With divine intervention ... redemption comes to the angels by way of salvation ... and Dick Turpin!

Late, early morning, York City Centre ... Julia has left her friends after spending a night wining and dancing and makes her way on foot to a taxi rank ...

She passes two young men in the opposite direction who whistle at her ...

Julia smiles ...

Suddenly, a white van passes on the other side of the road and pulls over abruptly into a side street on the left.

A man in a black hoodie jumps out and pulls her towards the van ...

Julia is bundled into the back ...

Julia screams ... and the two young men who passed her run towards the van.

"Help ... please someone help me" shouts Julia

The two young men turn to see the abduction and one of them manages to kick the side of the van. One of them makes a note of the number plate ...

An hour earlier ... inside the Ye Olde Starr Inne ... the main block of the pub is a timber framed structure, and it was constructed in the mid 16th century.

Another part of the building was erected in 1600.

In 1664 it was known as The Starre and it was part of a coaching yard, just off the northside of Stonegate.

The pub is steeped in history …

Julia and her friends, Sam, Natalie, and Sarah are all out on the town in celebration of her birthday.

"Well girls, what can I get you?" asks the Landlord

"We'll have …" advises Julia

Suddenly, someone else steps into order …

"For the lady a gnt" says the voice

"Why it's" says Natalie

"Mike Delaney" advises Sarah

"Don't you mean Professor Delaney?" asks Julia

"How are you, Mike?" asks Julia

Mike Delaney is an eminent Professor in York …

"What about us?" asks Sarah

The Landlord returns with the large gnt …

"Sorry, where are my manners, get the girls whatever they wish" advises Delaney

"Coming right up" says the Landlord

The pub is now almost full to the brim and becoming rowdy …

Police Detective Paul Mariner is close by with a young constable …

"You get all sorts in here, Jackson" advises Mariner

A couple start to come out of the pub and are both slightly the worse for wear …

"See what I mean?" advises Mariner

"Yes, Sir "says the young constable

After a couple of pints, Mariner and Jackson leave the pub …

John Paul is on his way back to the Bar Convent and walks by the pub

...

"Excuse me Sir" asks Mariner

John Paul stops in his tracks ...

"Don't I know you?" asks Mariner

"Have we met before?" asks John Paul

"You look familiar "responds Mariner

"Do I?" asks John Paul

"Then, maybe we have" advises John Paul

"Come on Jackson" advises Mariner

John Paul continues his way home to the Bar Convent, then hears a young woman in distress ...

"Help ...please someone help me" shouts a voice

John Paul rushes to the scene and sees a burly man pulling the girl towards a white van. John Paul rushes over to stop him but loses his grip ... Two young men also try to stop the moving van ...

John Paul disappears ...

A full-scale Police operation is now in progress ...

It's all over the News channels and being broadcast locally and internationally ...

GIRL ABDUCTED IN THE CENTRE OF YORK

The missing young woman, Julia, is 20 years old and a student at York University ... blonde, 5ft 8 ... anyone seeing this girl please contact the Police ...

"Typical Police procedure" advises a reporter

"Who is on the case?" asks the York Press Editor

"They have put Carmichael on it and DS Mariner"

"OK Riley, contact the DS and see what you can get for us" asks the Editor

"On to it Boss" responds the reporter

Back at York central Police Station the two young men who witnessed the abduction of Julia are now being questioned …

Inspector Carmichael is a typical down to earth Policeman, in his mid-forties, has light brown hair and blue eyes, but a plodder when it comes to Police investigations …

Paul Clarkson and Mick Naylor are in their early twenties …

"OK lads, tell me, what you told my Sergeant" advises Carmichael

Both start to tell their stories …

"OK … one at a time" asks Carmichael

"If we had only been a few minutes earlier" advises Mick

"Did you see anyone else at the scene?" asks Carmichael

"At the time of the abduction?" asks Carmichael

DS Mariner enters the room and whispers into the Inspectors ear …

Mariner is in his late thirties, has jet black hair and piercing green eyes, like his mentor, he is also a plodder but a stickler at getting to grips with the truth …

"Do you remember anything?" asks Carmichael

"Come to think of it, yes … another man" advises Paul

"Come to think of it?" asks Mariner

"OK, go on" says The Inspector

Paul begins to describe John Paul …

"Well, do we believe them, Sir?" asks Mariner

"I remember him too" advises Mariner

"How?" asks the Inspector

"I bumped into him coming out of the Starre Inne" advises Mariner

"Do you know who he is?" asks the Inspector

"Yes … and I know where we can find him too" advises Mariner

"How?" asks the Inspector

"We have bumped into each other a few times before" advises Mariner

"Do you know his name?" asks the Inspector

"He is known as … John Paul" advises Mariner

"John Paul who?" asks the Inspector

"I don't know his other name, but I know where he is staying" says Mariner

"The Bar Convent" advises Mariner

"OK then, make it snappy Mariner, bring him in for questioning" advises the Inspector

The Detective Sergeant makes a visit to the Bar Convent and detains John Paul as per orders …

"What's this all about?" asks John Paul

"Let's just say, we need you to help with our inquiries" says Mariner

"Can't it be done here?" asks John Paul

Nicola enters the meeting between John Paul and the detective Sergeant …

"What's going on?" asks Nicola

"I have been asked to attend, told to attend Police HQ in York for questioning" advises John Paul

"In what respect?" asks Nicola

"To help us in our inquiries" advises Mariner

"What's it to you?" asks Mariner

"I am John Paul's Solicitor, his brief, whatever you want to call it" advises Nicola

"Is this true?" asks Mariner

John Paul nods his head …

"Rather convenient, you also being here?" asks Mariner

"Don't be impertinent … now have you read John Paul his rights?"

asks Nicola

The DS starts to get agitated and begins to make mistakes …

"He's not under arrest" *advises Mariner*

"Is he under suspicion then?" *asks Nicola*

"Neither" *advises Mariner*

"Who is your Inspector?" *asks Nicola*

"Jack Carmichael" *advises Mariner*

"Well, as you are taking my client in for questioning, I will accompany you to the station" *advises Nicola*

"Yes, Miss?" *replies Mariner*

"What is your name?" *asks Mariner*

"Nicola Myers" *advises Nicola*

"What are the charges?" *asks Nicola*

"As I said there are no charges" *advises Mariner*

"Very well … will you co-operate with the Police?" *asks Nicola*

"Yes, I have nothing to hide" *advises John Paul*

Nicola and John Paul accompany DS Mariner to York Police HQ.

The Police car arrives at Fulford Road, which is just outside of the city.

The duty Sergeant whispers into DS Mariner's ear …

"We have looked at all the CCTV camera recordings in the area, at the time of the young woman's abduction, including when you met John Paul" *advises the duty Sergeant*

"And?" *asks Mariner*

"When you say you met John Paul …" *says the duty Sergeant*

"Yes … go on man" *advises Mariner*

"There is only your image on the camera footage" *advises the duty Sergeant*

"What do you mean ... only my image?" asks Mariner

"Yours is the only image on the video" repliesthe duty Sergeant

Nicola steps in asking for an update concerning her client ...

"Is there a problem Sergeant?" asks Nicola

"No ... no problem ... this way please" advises Mariner

The duty Sergeant looks daggers at Mariner and rolls his eyes ...

DS Mariner leads Nicola and John Paul into an Interview room with Inspector Carmichael waiting in the wings ...

"So, on what grounds and what evidence do you have concerning my client?" asks Nicola

"Client?" asks Carmichael

"I am Nicola Myers, duty Solicitor, duty Counsellor or duty Lawyer if you wish" advises Nicola

"Duty Lawyer from where?" asks Carmichael

"The Home Office" answers Nicola

"You mean?" asks Mariner

"Yes, exactly ... now what evidence do you have with regards my client?" asks Nicola

DS Mariner whispers into the Inspector's ear ...

"I'm afraid, we owe you both an apology" says Carmichael

"I take it, this is all to do with the abduction of a young woman in the city?" asks John Paul

"Yes" confirms Carmichael

"Maybe we can pool our resources and work together on this?" advises Nicola

"Can you help us?" asks the Inspector

"We have our ways" advises Nicola

"OK, your free to go" says the Inspector

The duty Sergeant enters the Interview room and advises about another case …

All are astonished at what the duty Sergeant is saying.

"Dick Turpin, the highwayman in York?" asks Carmichael

"The ghost of Dick Turpin?" asks Mariner

"You must be joking, right?" asks the Inspector

"It's no joke, Sir" advises the duty Sergeant

"Would you like our assistance?" asks John Paul

"Well, I am truly flummoxed about this" says Carmichael

"How can you help us?" asks Mariner

"We will investigate, and see what we can do" says Nicola

"Where did the sighting take place?" asks John Paul

"According to the witness … on the Knavesmire" advises the duty Sergeant

"Where is that?" asks John Paul

"The site is now occupied by York racecourse" advises Mariner

"It's not far from the Bar Convent" replies John Paul

"Will you want our assistance?" asks Carmichael

"Let us see just exactly what we are up against first" advises Nicola

"… and the abduction?" asks John Paul

"We may be able to help with that too" advises Nicola

"How?" asks Mariner

"We have our ways of locating people" says Nicola

"We'll be in touch" says John Paul

PART 2 - THE RETURN
OF DICK TURPIN?

Ater living a notorious life, Richard Turpin, moved to York and assumed the alias of John Palmer.

He was, in fact, a legendary highwayman and his involvement with crime is synonymous with his fame ... but York would prove to be his downfall!

When a sighting on the Knavesmire comes to the attention of the Angel's, and the abduction of Julia in the city also takes a different turn, divine intervention may be needed to help the investigation.

Nicola and John Paul ask for help ...

Leeds city centre, 2nd Floor, Angel's Eyes Investigations.

Rebecca and Mary are in conversation with Kate and Peter ...

"We've found something interesting to investigate" advises Kate

"Our client is trying to locate someone they met at a Single's dance in Leeds" advises Peter

"Singles Dance?" asks Mary

"You know ... where boy meets girl" advises Rebecca

"How can we help them, Rebecca?" asks Mary

"The file says the person is known to go there often" advises Kate

"Strange case ... how can we help?" asks Mary

"We've been asked to persuade them to return to their partner" advises Peter

"And if they don't?" asks Mary

"That's the job ... do we take it or not?" asks Kate

"OK ... we'll do it" advises Rebecca

"What about Peter?" asks Mary

"What about me?" asks Peter

Peter advises that he will act as their escort and accompany them to the Singles dance as back up.

"Just in case you get into any trouble" advises Peter

"How?" asks Rebecca

"Wait and see" advises Peter

The New Venture Singles Dance is a weekly get together for men and women in Leeds at the 4-star Metropole Hotel in King Street in the city centre.

The Hotel is a Grade 2 listed building, it opened in 1899.

Thursday evening, 9pm ... lobby/entrance to the Metropole Hotel, in the foyer.

Kate, Peter, Mary, and Rebecca are dressed for the occasion.

"I'll find out where the dance is taking place" advises Peter

Peter checks with reception then returns to advise the news.

"The Singles Dance is in the ballroom, straight in front of us" advises Peter

Music can be heard playing in the background to get everyone in the mood.

"Good evening" says a gentleman at the door

"Hi" says Kate

"Are all four of you joining us tonight?" asks the doorman

"Why are you all coming apart?" asks Mary

Lots of laughing now takes place ...

"Very funny" advises the doorman

"My name is Brian ... I like someone with a good sense of humour" laughs Brian

Mary blushes at her laughable comments.

"Sorry Brian, it's our first time" advises Rebecca

"That is OK ... but if old style music hall ever comes back, I will be sure to recommend you to the City Varieties" replies Brian

"City Varieties?" asks Mary

"That's another story, Mary" advises Kate

"Thank you" replies Peter

"Maybe I'll see you later, Miss?" asks Brian

"Mary, my name's Mary" is the reply

"Look forward to it Mary" advises Brian

Peter guides Mary, Kate, and Rebecca into the ballroom.

"You were quite the flirt, Mary" advises Peter

"Flirt?" asks Mary

"Rebecca, I will let you explain that one to Mary" asks Peter

Kate finds a table for four and they are all just about to sit down when someone comes forward to try their luck.

"Can I have this dance, pretty lady?" says a voice

"We've only just got here" advises Kate

"What a compliment" says Mary

"Compliment?" asks Rebecca

"Yes, of course, I would love to" replies Mary

"Remember, Mary" advises Rebecca

"Remember what?" asks Mary

"We're here on business, not pleasure" replies Rebecca

"I'll remember" advises Mary

"Don't worry Rebecca, I will keep my eye on her" advises Peter

"She may need rescuing at some point" responds Kate

"How?" asks Rebecca

"Well, I have the perfect plan" advises Peter

"Wait and see" says Peter

"Now, exactly, who are we looking for Kate?" asks Rebecca

Kate produces a photograph from the file.

"This is the man, Peter Quinn" advises Kate

"Remind me again, why we are investigating him?" asks Rebecca

"His wife suspects he is cheating on her" advises Kate

"His wife?" asks Rebecca

"I didn't realise we would be investigating such matters" replies Rebecca

"OK ... we'll keep our eyes peeled" says Peter

"Eyes peeled?" asks Rebecca

"It's just a way of saying we will keep a look out, Rebecca" advises Peter

The music changes to loud disco and the beat gets Rebecca's feet tapping.

"May I have this dance?" asks a young man

"Kate is the dancer ... I am just an observer" replies Rebecca

"For an observer you are quite stunning" says the young man

Rebecca blushes and smiles at the young man.

Kate accepts the request, and she manages to persuade Rebecca to go on the dance floor.

Another man starts to chat up Rebecca and she decides to go on to the floor to keep her cover.

"So, do you come here often?" asks the man

"No, first time" answers Rebecca

"My name is Sam" advises the young man

"I am Rebecca" is the reply

"So where have you been all my life?" asks Sam

Rebecca smiles and accepts the compliment.

"I like your pretty dress ... you smell like cookies" advises Sam

"Cookies?" asks Rebecca

"Rather sweet" says Sam

"Is that supposed to be a joke?" asks Rebecca

"No, it wasn't meant to be" advises Sam

"You really do smell heavenly" replies the young man

"Were you wafted here from paradise?" asks Sam

"Maybe" smiles Rebecca

Back in York, John Paul, and Nicola head to the Knavesmire on the racecourse in search of the legendary highwayman, Dick Turpin.

Night is beginning to fall and the Knavesmire is a marsh undeveloped area which is also known as the stray. It was also one of four public execution sites in York and it was used up until 1801.

Suddenly, a white van turns up. The driver gets out and releases an occupant from the rear of the van. They are covered in a black bin liner and tied up.

John Paul and Nicola rush over to the scene.

John Paul removes the bin liner to reveal the victim is Alex, another missing young woman who also disappeared off the streets of York a year ago.

"Are you alright?" asks John Paul

Nicola removes the gag from the girl's mouth.

The young woman is in shock. Nicola contacts DS Mariner.

The Police arrive on the scene in a blaze of blue lights and wailing sirens ...

The area is quickly cordoned off and medical teams are on hand.

"Is it Julia?" asks Mariner

A police officer rushes over to help the medical staff.

"No … my name is Alex" replies the shocked young woman

"I'm afraid she is in shock" advises John Paul

A doctor arrives on the scene and begins to treat Alex.

"Just a minute" advises Mariner

"Do you remember anything, Alex?" asks Mariner

"Yes, some details" advises Alex

"OK, we will go into those later" advises Mariner

A white bright light suddenly appears and, in the background, can be seen a man on horseback.

"Who is it?" asks Nicola

"It looks like Dick Turpin" advises Mariner

"Who is Dick Turpin?" asks Nicola

"He was a famous legendary highwayman" advises John Paul

"Why is he here, on the Knavesmire?" asks Nicola

"This is where he was hanged in 1739" advises Mariner

"The 7ᵗʰ of April" responds John Paul

"You're very well informed on our history" responds Mariner

"Just a passing interest" advises John Paul

"He's on the run" replies Mariner

"On the run from whom?" asks Nicola

"He was known as John Palmer. He became York's most notorious prisoner, the legendary highwayman, Dick Turpin" advises Mariner

The figure is on horseback, suddenly leaves a clue on the Knavesmire, then disappears.

"The ghost of Dick Turpin" advises Mariner

"Some say he is alive again, and carrying out various matters in York" informs Mariner

"As a ghost?" asks John Paul

"Yes, precisely" replies Mariner

"He was imprisoned in York Castle" advises Mariner

"York castle?" asks John Paul

A young Police constable brings over the clue to DS Mariner.

"Thank you, Patchett" replies Mariner

"What is it?" asks John Paul

"It looks like part of a woman's dress" advises Mariner

"Julia's?" asks Nicola

"How?" asks John Paul

"Maybe Dick Turpin has turned over a new leaf helping the Police" responds Nicola

"Today … in 2023? … I think it highly unlikely" advises Mariner

"Never underestimate the power of the spirit" advises John Paul

"What else can you tell us about Dick Turpin?" asks John Paul

York Castle has been a site of justice and incarceration for almost a thousand years. It is still a seat of justice today.

The 18th century building is now York Crown Court.

"Do you think he can help us find Julia?" asks Nicola

"Well, the clue he left behind may help us. We will check it for DNA" advises Mariner

"Look at this" advises John Paul

"What have you found?" asks Nicola

"A ghost tour of the Castle Museum is due to take place later tonight" advises John Paul

"Ghost tour?" asks Mariner

"I think we had better check it out" advises Nicola

"We'll rendezvous with you later DS Mariner" advises John Paul

"OK, I will get our people to check into the DNA and I will advise you if it does belong to Julia" advises Mariner

DS Mariner leaves the scene and proceeds back to York Police HQ.

A comprehensive test with the sample garment may produce the results DS Mariner is looking for, but will it also contain the DNA of Dick Turpin?

Nicola and John Paul are not left on the Knavesmire alone.

"Do you think divine intervention is playing a part here?" asks Nicola

"More than likely, Nicola" advises John Paul "Maybe it is a way of salvation … and somehow Dick Turpin is part of it" replies John Paul

PART 3 - ILLUMINATION
AND FACING FACTS

York city centre, the anniversary ghost tour at the Castle Museum.

John Paul, Nicola, and Joseph encounter the eerie ghost of Dick Turpin and are asked for redemption by several unsavoury characters.

When the lights go out at the famous Castle Museum stories of the prison's illuminating past are told by experienced staff.

They tell of gruesome punishments, inflicted harrowing executions for those found guilty and tales of the paranormal witnessed by staff members in recent years. Themes of torture, death, and assault.

York Castle Museum, "Ghost" tour, Saturday, 8pm ... John Paul, Nicola, and Joseph congregate in the foyer awaiting the Tour Guide.

"So, is this the place?" asks Nicola

"Why has it been set up as a museum?" asks John Paul

"Things happen here" advises Joseph

"Things?" asks Nicola

"Unexplained happenings, phenomenon" advises Joseph

"Can you elaborate any further?" asks John Paul

"There have been reports of numerous ghostly apparitions here, along with doors slamming by unseen hands" advises Joseph

"Unseen hands?" asks Nicola

The Tour Guide arrives and starts to elaborate further to those who are on the ghost tour.

"Good evening, my name is Ben" says the voice

"You may encounter heavy footsteps and drastic air temperature changes on the tour" advises Ben

"Ghosts?" asks a tourist

"Yes, ghosts" confirms Ben

"They are just some of the unexplained occurrences that happen here" insists Ben

"Tonight, you have all been specially invited on a natural and intense ghost hunt at the haunted York Castle Museum" advises Ben

"Don't you mean, with special effects?" asks a tourist

"I can assure you there are no special effects here. What you will see, and encounter is real" advises Ben

"We will all spend the night together, in vigil, to see who still haunts this old, haunted castle" insists Ben

"York Castle is said to be the most haunted museum in the UK" advises Ben

"The location is hidden with an old 18th century prison home to highwaymen and murderers" informs Ben

"Are you all ready to begin our ghost hunt?" asks Ben

"What about Dick Turpin?" asks a tourist

"Wasn't he imprisoned here?" asks another tourist

"Indeed, he was and executed on the Knavesmire" advises Ben

"We start here … Kirkgate" advises Ben

"As you can see it is a replica Victorian street!" advises Ben

"An exact replica?" asks Nicola

"Yes" advises Joseph

"It is one of the oldest and it became a centre piece of the museum when it opened in 1938" advises Ben

"I remember it" advises Nicola

"Remember … how?" asks Joseph

"What Nicola means is that she remembers it from her old college days" says John Paul

The Tour Guide walks on with the rest of the tourists.

"Why have we stopped here?" asks Joseph

"I can feel it … can you Nicola?" advises John Paul

"Feel it … feel what?" asks Joseph

The rumbling of horse's hooves can be heard, and a bright shining light illuminates where they are. In its wake a ghostly figure is on horseback.

"Why it's …" says Nicola

"Dick Turpin" advises John Paul

"On black Bess" replies Joseph

"It can't be" says Joseph

The ghostly figure stands silent in a ghostly mist and motionless.

John Paul calls out to Turpin.

"You are Dick Turin?" asks John Paul

The ghostly figure is rigid and offers no response.

"Let me try" says Nicola

"Be my guest" advises John Paul

"Highwayman, why are you here?" asks Nicola

"Highwayman?" replies Turpin

"Who are you?" asks Turpin

"I am Nicola, this is John Paul and Joseph" replies Nicola

"I sense you're not of this World" asks Turpin

"What does he mean?" asks Joseph

"You are Dick Turpin, aren't you?" asks John Paul

"Well?" asks Nicola

"I am he" replies Turpin

"Why did you help the Police concerning the missing girl?" asks Nicola

Turpin does not respond and continues to be motionless.

"The Police advise the note from the Knavesmire is to do with Julia, the missing young woman" asks John Paul

"I know where she is" advises Turpin

"Can you locate her for us?" asks Nicola

"Wrong question, Nicola" advises John Paul

"Can you take us to her?" asks John Paul

"For a price" advises Turpin

"A price?" asks John Paul

"Name it" advises Nicola

"I am forever stuck here in time" says Turpin

"We can help you" advises Nicola

"You are not of this World, are you?" asks Turpin

"We are from another time, another place" advises John Paul

"Time … place?" asks Turpin

Joseph continues to ask questions.

Nicola touches Joseph on the arm and his memory is erased of present events.

"We will meet your price, highwayman" advises John Paul

Back in Leeds, at the Metropole Hotel, Rebecca and Mary seem to be getting themselves into a pickle at the Singles Dance.

"Where are you from Rebecca?" asks Sam

"Leeds" replies Rebecca

"You?" asks Rebecca

"Leeds" advises Sam

"Snap" says Sam

"Do you know of a man called Peter Quinn?" asks Rebecca

"No, I don't think so, but maybe the organisers will know him" replies Sam

Sam pulls Rebecca towards him for a kiss.

Suddenly, someone intervenes. Peter to the rescue.

"So, this is where you are" asks Peter

"Who are you?" asks Sam

"Oh, didn't Rebecca tell you ... I am her husband" replies Peter

"Well, no I am sorry" responds Sam

Sam apologises and leaves for the bar area.

"Sorry to break that up Rebecca. I thought you needed rescuing" advises Peter

"You thought right, Peter" replies Rebecca

"Another minute ..." says Rebecca

"And the game would have been up" advises Mary

"Game?" asks Peter

"Mary's subtle way of humour" advises Rebecca

"Did you ask about Peter Quinn?" asks Kate

"As a matter of fact, I did" replies Rebecca

"What did he tell you?" asks Peter

"Sam believed that the organisers would know him" advises Rebecca

"The doorman?" asks Peter

"Apparently, he is the most likely one to know" replies Rebecca

"OK, I will go over and question him" advises Peter

"No Peter, I will go" advises Rebecca

"I have got myself into trouble enough for one night. I will see what I can find out" replies Rebecca

"You all continue to enjoy yourselves here" advises Rebecca

Rebecca chats to the doorman at length.

"Hi, remember me?" asks Rebecca

"How can I forget?" is the response

"I am Rebecca" says the voice

"Terry" advises the doorman

"I wonder if you can help me?" asks Rebecca

"I will try" advises Terry

"I am looking for a man called Peter Quinn. Do you know him?" asks Rebecca

"Are you Police?" asks Terry

"No … we are investigators" advises Rebecca

"Why do you want to know about Peter?" asks Terry

"His wife says he is cheating on her" replies Rebecca

"His wife?" asks Terry

"Now, I understand. We run a strict policy here for Singles only. Here are his details" advises Terry

"Thank you, Terry" replies Rebecca

Rebecca returns to the table where Mary, Kate, and Peter are seated.

"How did you get on Rebecca?" asks Mary

"Got it, address, everything" replies Rebecca

"What if he is shacked up with someone else?" asks Peter

"Shacked up?" asks Mary

"Living with someone else" advises Peter

"Now I get it ... shacked up" replies Mary

"We will deal with that as and when we need to" advises Rebecca

"When?" asks Kate

"Well, there is no time like the present" advises Rebecca

Kate, Peter, Mary, and Rebecca leave the Metropole Hotel in King Street only to find two cars have collided leaving one on its roof with several occupants trapped inside.

"We will go for help" advise Mary and Rebecca

Peter takes out his mobile and begins to dial 999.

"Emergency ... what service do you require?" asks the operator

"Ambulance responder fast ... and you'd better send the fire brigade too" asks Peter

"Where?" asks the operator

"Just outside the Metropole Hotel on King Street. Two cars have collided with several occupants trapped inside. One of the vehicles is beginning to smoulder" advises Peter

"Fire and rescue on their way. Ambulance responder already dispatched and with you, eta 4 minutes" advises the operator

Peter continues to give more details of the crash and current situation.

Mary and Rebecca return disguised as Ambulance Responder crew.

"The Fire and rescue and Police are on their way" advises Peter

"When did it happen?" asks a responder

"I don't know, I just got here" advises Peter

"There looks to be a few injured" says a responder

"OK, we will have to be quick" says Rebecca

Luckily, the door of the overturned car is open, and a couple of *occupants manage to climb out of the vehicle unscathed.*

"Are you both alright?" asks Mary

"You have both had a miraculous escape" advises Rebecca

"Can you help Tom?" asks one of the passengers

"Tom, our driver?" asks a young lady

"I think he has passed out" advises another young lady

"OK, please step back onto the pavement" is the response

"It looks like he has had a cardiac arrest" advises Rebecca

"We need to act fast" replies Mary

Sirens can be heard in the background.

A sudden bright beam of light fills the inside of the car.

"What's happening?" asks the young woman

"What's your name?" asks Peter

"Cheryl" replies the young woman

"OK ... I am Peter ... they know what they are doing ... and are probably illuminating the inside of the car to help your friend" advises Peter

Peter places his jacket around Cheryl. She is in shock.

"Tom, can you hear me?" asks Rebecca

Tom suddenly awakes to find no one around him, and he climbs out of the car.

"What happened?" asks Tom

The Police, Emergency Responder and Fire crew are now all on the scene.

"What's the story?" asks someone from the press

"All I remember is someone helping me, a bright light, then feeling cured. I have no pain at all" advises Tom

"Angels?" asks the reporter

"What do you mean, Angels?" asks a Police officer

The Reporter produces several feathers found near the overturned vehicle.

"Can all of this really be true?" asks the reporter

PART 4 - DIVINE INTERVENTION

In the finale, John Paul, Nicola, and Joseph encounter Dick Turpin's ghost and are hot on the heels of the missing girl.

Rebecca and Mary journey to York to help and salvation comes by way of an unknown source.

The Editor's office, York Evening Post Newpapers.

"What on earth is going on?" asks the Editor

The Editor is in a meeting with various reporters covering the missing girl story.

"OK, we have all been given priority by the board of directors concerning the recent angel happenings in the city" advises the Editor

"What have you got Mark?" asks the Editor

"Several witness statements confirming sightings and divine intervention" advises the reporter

"Divine intervention?" asks the Editor

"We've also been given several endorsements" advises the reporter

"Where?" asks the Editor

"Our sources in the city" adds the reporter

"Can they identify who we need to track down?" asks the Editor

"Yes, but they are suspicious of any activity and are afraid" informs the reporter

"Afraid, exactly of what?" asks the Editor

The Reporter starts to go into fine detail with the Editor and his colleagues.

Meanwhile in the centre of York, John Paul, Nicola, and Joseph are investigating into yet another case concerning missing persons.

They meet the client, Luke Parsons, along Whip-ma-Whop-Ma-Gate, one of the shortest streets in York ...

"What an unusual name for a street" advises John Paul

"What does it mean, Joseph?" asks Nicola

"According to York's history it is the shortest street and from 1505 the meaning was known as what a street" advises Joseph

"What a street indeed" replies John Paul

"What a street?" asks Nicola

"Sorry Joseph, I just don't understand" advises Nicola

The street in question is to be found at the end of the Shambles and at the intersection of where Collier Gate and Fosgate meet.

Suddenly, a young man with a shock of blond hair arrives on the scene.

"Joseph?" asks the young man

"Yes, I am Joseph" is the response

"Luke Parsons ... we spoke on the phone" advises the young man

"Welcome Luke, may I present John Paul and Nicola" asks Joseph

"How may we help you?" asks John Paul

"The missing girl" advises Luke

"What about the missing girl?" asks Nicola

"I have news" advises Luke

"Go on" asks John Paul

"I know where she is ... and who is holding her" advises Luke

"Why have you not gone to the Police with this information?" asks Joseph

"No Police" insists Luke

"OK, you've got our attention Luke ... we are listening" advises John Paul

"Tonight 8pm near the Jorvik centre ... come alone" advises Luke

"Why the urgency, Luke?" asks John Paul

"Come alone ... and remember no Police" insists Luke

"Until then" advises Luke

Luke suddenly disappears into the crowds of shoppers and tourists.

"I don't like it, John Paul" advises Joseph

"Why?" asks Nicola

"Somehow, I feel it may be a trap" insists Joseph

"We will ask Rebecca and Mary to join us tonight plus Peter and Kate" says Nicola

"Why are you getting involved?" asks Joseph

"Because we have to" advises Nicola

"And the Police?" asks Joseph

"We may need their help too" advises Joseph

"In what way?" asks John Paul

"You'll see" advises Joseph

"We may need to create a diversion" advises Nicola

"An illusion, Joseph?" asks John Paul

"Don't worry, we will handle it" advises Nicola

Back in Leeds, Rebecca, Mary, Kate, and Peter are tying up loose ends concerning a previous investigation.

"What do you think, Mary?" asks Rebecca

Kate enters the room with refreshments.

"I think we have got a problem" advises Mary

"A problem?" asks Rebecca

"In what way?" asks Mary

"Remember the Monsignor from St Anne's Cathedral" asks Kate

"Yes, we remember" advises Mary

"I have just checked the CCTV footage with our security company" advises Kate

"Yes, what did they find?" asks Rebecca

"The Monsignor looks to be gathering information and evidence against you for the Bishop" advises Kate

"Evidence?" asks Mary

"What Kate means is that they are checking us out" advises Peter

"Checking us out?" asks Mary

"Don't worry" says Peter

"I will deal with it … I have a plan to throw them off course" advises Peter

"Yes, I will too" advises Kate

"Thank you both" replies Rebecca

"We will simply put them on to another trail" advises Peter

"How?" asks Rebecca

"A smokescreen" replies Peter

"Smokescreen?" asks Mary

"Something to satisfy their curiosity" advises Kate

Rebecca advises they have all been summoned to York to help John Paul and Nicola with an investigation.

"We need to travel to York" advises Rebecca

"Are we needed there?" asks Mary

"Yes" advises Rebecca

"Where?" asks Mary

"The Jorvik Viking centre" replies Rebecca

"John Paul and Nicola have asked for our help concerning a missing young woman" advises Rebecca

Later, early evening, York city centre.

John Paul, Nicola, Rebecca, Mary, Joseph, Peter, and Kate are all gathered together at a place near to the Jorvik Viking Centre.

They encounter someone tied up, their head has been covered with sackcloth.

John Paul removes the sackcloth from the victim.

"Why it's" says Peter

"Julia ... the missing young woman" responds Nicola

Another male person steps out from the shadows.

"You" says John Paul

"Professor Delaney" warns Nicola

"Mike Delaney" responds the voice

Luke also steps out of the shadows.

"I told you I would bring you more than just the girl" advises Luke

"Delaney" says Luke

"What about Delaney?" asks Nicola

"He's your man" insists Luke

"Why?" asks Kate

No response from the Professor. He stands still as if rooted to the ground.

"You see Professor Delaney is in need of help … quite insane" informs Luke

"A split personality?" asks Mary

"Yes, very much so" advises Luke

A sudden shock of light emerges … the ghostly figure of the Centurian with his cohort of guards reappear.

"Agmen formante" says the Centurian

The soldiers are ordered to form a square formation by the Centurian.

"We meet again, Centurian" says John Paul

The Centurian responds "Ciringite frontem" which is the command for "Maintain position" advises the Centurian

"Centurian why have you disobeyed orders?" asks Nicola

The Centurian remains silent and stands rigid.

"Answer the question" asks John Paul

"We have not disobeyed orders … we are legionnaires" advises the Centurian

"Centurian, why are you here?" asks Nicola

"To deliver the lost soul" answers the Centurian

"Lost soul?" asks Mary

"He means return the missing young woman, Julia" advises John Paul

"What about Professor Delaney?" asks Joseph

"You could say he has been frightened out of his wits" advises John Paul

"I will agree with that" advises Kate

"I didn't think we would encounter such beings during this investigation" advises Rebecca

Another bright light emerges, and the ghostly form of Dick Turpin reappears on his horse, black Bess.

"Why, it's Dick Turpin" advises Peter

"The famous Highwayman" says Joseph

"Divine intervention?" asks Rebecca

"Redemption, salvation and Dick Turpin" advises John Paul

"Centurian, where do you go now?" asks John Paul

"Front Allargate" answers the Centurian

The Centurian gives the command to the cohort to disperse positions.

"God speed" advises John Paul

"Te cambre" answers the Centurian

The Centurian gives the command to leave, and the cohort disappears through a wall.

Dick Turpin's ghostly form waves and returns into the ghostly mist.

"It's all over" advises John Paul

The Police arrive on the scene and take control of the situation.

DS Mariner talks to John Paul about the investigation and Julia's return.

"I still don't understand how you managed to find Julia" asks Mariner

"Call it a feeling, call it what you will, I suppose we had luck on our *side" advises John Paul*

"Much more than luck I would say" advises Nicola

"When you come to think of it" replies Peter

"We're just happy to see that Julia has been found" responds Rebecca

"And you are?" asks Mariner

"Rebecca and Mary are our associates from our Leeds office" advises John Paul

"Kate and Peter are also from Leeds" advises Nicola

"So, it was a joint operation?" asks Mariner

"Yes, you could call it that" responds Nicola

"Thank you for all your help" advises Mariner

"Well, if we can be of any further assistance?" asks Mariner

"There may be one or two things that you could help us with" advises Nicola

"Just let me know" insists Mariner

Next day in Leeds and York, the Police have put a black out on the news concerning the missing young woman, Julia.

As for the Press and the Church pursuing the angels, they too have been dismissed … but will their eventual curiosity get the better of them?

Meanwhile, at the most haunted pub in York, the Golden Fleece on the pavement, a ghost is present in the form of one-eyed Jack

who wears a 16th century Redcoat and carries a pistol. He has appeared in a downstairs cellar.

Spooky encounters and ghosts roam the Snickelways and haunt Georgian town houses and historical inns all over the city.

York is affectionately known as the ancient city of 1,000 ghosts.

It certainly lives up to its name!

There are stories to be found anywhere.

York's reputation is known Worldwide.

DECREE AND RESOLUTION

PART ONE – LOOKING

FOR ANSWERS

When the angels take on a complex investigation in Leeds assisting Marie, a local clairvoyant, track down several hauntings' attention forms and they become a best-selling story with the press.

High drama at the Thackray Medical Museum calls the angels together in the wake of ghostly apparitions.

In York, Nicola and John Paul come face to face with several notorious hauntings. They are unaware of their link to the Leeds investigations.

At the same time, the Press and Church are investigating into the unusual phenomenon in Leeds and York. They are trying to find evidence regarding the existence of the angels and to expose them to the World.

When help comes from an unlikely source, decree and resolution comes together at the end of both investigations.

PARK SQUARE, LEEDS, ANGEL'S EYES INVESTIGATIONS OFFICE SUITE, 2ND FLOOR …

Kate informs Rebecca and Mary of their next investigation …

The bell rings …

"Why it's Samantha" advises Mary

"Welcome Samantha, come in, how are you?" greets Rebecca

"I'm fine, I was wondering" asks Samantha

"Wondering about what?" asks Mary

Kate leaves to make the coffee. Samantha continues her story.

"I've received an unusual request" advises Samantha

"Unusual in what way?" asks Rebecca

Samantha advises her version of events and the story of a recent occurrence.

"You have got our attention Samantha, how can we help you?" asks

Mary

Samantha continues to relay her complex story.

"It concerns several hauntings at the Thackray Medical Museum"
advises Samantha

"Hauntings?" asks Mary

"My contact informs me that many ghosts and ghouls are rumoured
to be wandering around the museum and when the lights go out the
location has a real story to tell" informs Samantha

"How can we help you?" asks Rebecca

The Thackray Medical Museum sits in the grounds of one of
the largest workhouses in Leeds. It was opened in 1861 and
was originally built as the former Leeds Union Workhouse and
accommodated over 784 paupers.

The building is situated in the grounds of St. James Hospital.

"St James again" advises Mary

"What do you mean?" asks Samantha

"It's just Mary's way of thinking" advises Rebecca

"Who has asked for the investigation to be carried out?" asks Mary

"Living relatives" advises Samantha

"What's their interest?" asks Rebecca

"A prominent level of paranormal activity has been witnessed there
by the Museum staff. We have been instructed to investigate" advises
Samantha

Kate re-enters the meeting with the coffees and starts to hand them
out.

"We?" asks Kate

Peter now also arrives in the office and enters the meeting.

"Have no fear ... Peter is here" says the voice

"Come in Peter" laughs Mary

"Marie this is Peter and Kate ... our business associates" advises Rebecca

"Sorry, did we miss something?" asks Peter

"Samantha was our first investigation" advises Rebecca

"She is now asking for our help at the Thackray Medical Museum" advises Rebecca

"The Thackray Museum is haunted" advises Peter

Samantha produces a file that has been compiled by several members of staff at the Museum. She begins to reel off what they have been up against.

"We may encounter dark figures roaming around the building, poltergeist activity, loud footsteps, whispers, crying, rapid drops in temperature ... and" advises Samantha

"Please continue" asks Rebecca

"People have been known to be touched and grabbed by unseen hands" informs Samantha

"That sounds very spooky" insists Kate

"I know what you're thinking ... is it all really true?" advises Samantha

"Everything has been verified" insists Samantha

"There have been witnesses who have seen electrical paranormal activity and electronic voice phenomenon" advises Samantha

"Read it for yourself ... it's all in the file" advises Samantha

Samantha hands the file to Rebecca.

"This is without doubt one location that seems to provide many unexplained experiences" advises Peter

"Are you afraid?" asks Samantha

"No, on the contrary, we are very intrigued" replies Rebecca

"Will you experience, in the dead of night, your haunted adventure at the Thackray Museum?" asks Samantha

"Just tell us where and when" advises Mary

"What about tomorrow night, if your able to make it?" asks Samantha

"OK we agree, we will help you in this investigation" advises Rebecca

Mary, Kate, and Peter also confirm they will accompany Rebecca and Samantha to the haunted museum.

In York, Nicola and John Paul are asked by the Police to help concerning unusual paranormal phenomena in the city centre.

The ancient city of York is well known for paranormal activity. A glut of ghostly happenings and locations have become part of York's legacy as much as the Vikings and Romans.

The Last Drop Inn, part of the Blacksheep Brewery, in Toft Green, York boasts several sightings of paranormal activity.

The building has a colourful past.

It was once a morgue then a vicarage before coming the brewery of today.

A spirit is said to stalk the Halls.

Detective Sergeant Mariner is in conversation with Nicola and John Paul at York Central Police Station.

"How can we help?" asks Nicola

"As you may well know, York is known for ghostly apparitions" advises Mariner

"We are aware" advises John Paul

"Staff have reported heavy footsteps at the Last Drop Inn" advises Mariner

"Last drop of what?" asks Nicola

"Beer" advises Mariner

"Tell us of the ghostly sightings" asks John Paul

"Readings have been reported to be way off the scale in temperature" advises Mariner

"Why have the Police been asked to investigate?" asks Nicola

"We have been charged with finding some ancient information that may tie in with one of our cases" advises Mariner

"In what way?" asks John Paul

"I am afraid that is classified ... but if you could help on behalf of the Police, we would be most grateful" advises Mariner

"OK, you have got our attention" replies Nicola

"We believe the paranormal activity at the Last Drop Inn ties in to a similar case at the Golden Fleece on the Pavement, in the city centre" advises Mariner

"In what way?" asks John Paul

"The Golden Fleece is known as York's most haunted pub, and one of the oldest dating back to 1503" advises Mariner

"So, why the investigation?" asks John Paul

"Home Office instructions" advises Mariner

"Wouldn't it be better if they had a specialised team leading the investigation?" asks Nicola

"We have been asked for local expertise on this matter" advises Mariner

John Paul and Nicola nod at each other.

"OK, we'll take on the case" advises Nicola

"We are intrigued. You will have to advise us all the intricate details" asks John Paul

Back in Leeds, Kate, Peter, Mary, Rebecca, and Samantha meet near the Thackray Medical Museum before the ghostly vigil.

Samantha begins to advise them of what lies ahead.

"There have been reported sightings of a nineteenth century woman known as the Gray Lady" informs Samantha

"The Gray Lady?" asks Rebecca

"We have encountered her before" advises Mary

"Where?" asks Samantha

"At the General Infirmary" advises Rebecca

"Can it be the same one?" asks Mary

"She used to walk the corridors of Leeds General Infirmary" advises Rebecca

"What happened here?" asks Peter

"She is also known to walk the wards with a white coated Doctor here at the Thackray Medical Museum" informs Samantha

"Rapid changes in temperature have also taken place" informs Samantha

"What about other evidence?" asks Peter

"The location has also provided lots of readings and evidence from various paranormal electronic equipment" advises Samantha

The clock strikes 8pm and they are suddenly joined by various members of the Museum Tour staff and other would be ghost hunters.

The team are friendly, deeply knowledgeable, and experienced paranormal operators.

"We are about to enter one of the UK's most haunted buildings, and we will try to communicate with its resident spirits and ghosts in the dark" informs a staff member.

"My name is Alex. I will be your guide for the evening"

"If anyone suffers from being in the dark now is the time to leave" advises Alex

"This is a real ghost hunt experience. There is no fakery or trickery of paranormal activity. What you see is what you get" advises Alex

"If anything happens, it happens for real" advises Alex

Alex checks her folder and then informs the group.

"OK, we will work as teams" advises Alex

Rebecca takes charge and advises Alex that Mary, Peter, Kate, and Samantha will form their team.

Another two teams are split and put together by Alex.

"You will all have maximum involvement" advises Alex

"Let me at those ghosts" shouts someone in the group

Everyone in the group laughs.

"Remember, be hands on" advises Alex

"You will have everything you need to help you throughout the night" informs Alex

"We have been given exclusive access to the Museum for our overnight ghost hunt" informs Alex

"We will all learn about various ghost hunting techniques. If you have any knowledge to share or process, we will use it in our investigation" advises Alex

"There are various gadgets at our disposal and up to date electronic equipment" informs Alex

"I've got to get my hands on that" advises Peter

"Very high tech" says Kate

"We will be in charge of that" advises Peter

"Your scientific vigil has begun" informs Alex

"You can take part or just be an observer … the choice is yours" says Alex

"How will it help us?" asks Peter

"You will learn how to apply spiritual protection" advises Alex

Rebecca and Mary already begin to detect something.

"Can you hear that?" asks Mary

"Yes" advises Rebecca

"I think it is coming from over there" advises Mary

Alex steps forward and begins to question their investigation.

"Have you detected something?" asks Alex

"We're not sure" advises Kate

"Do you have a reading?" asks Rebecca

Peter shakes the handheld machine.

"It appears to be off the scale here" says Peter

"Off the scale?" asks Kate

"Prepare for incoming" advises Peter

Back in York, Nicola and John Paul begin their paranormal investigation at The Golden Fleece in the city centre and are taken aback by their findings.

Can it really all be true?

PART 2 - PARANORMAL ACTIVITY

Inside The Thackray Medical Museum, Leeds.

Kate, Peter, Mary, Rebecca, and Samantha have taken on a case concerning paranormal activity and are about to taking part in an overnight vigil.

Back in York, Nicola and John Paul are likewise investigating a similar case which may coincide with the Leeds investigation.

"This was originally a workhouse" advises Alex

"Then it was known as the East Leeds War Hospital" continues Alex

"In 1925 the building became St. James Hospital" says Alex

"Jimmy's" says Kate

"Yes, Jimmy's" advises Alex

Peter advises readings of paranormal activity on the electrical equipment are fluctuating.

"The equipment is all over the place" advises Peter

"Have you got a fix?" asks Kate

"Whatever it is, it should be right ahead of us" informs Peter

"Where's Alex?" asks Rebecca

"She was here a minute ago" advises Mary

A ghostly figure steps out of an eery mist in front of them.

"Who are you?" asks Rebecca

The ghostly figure offers no response.

Peter switches on the tape recorder and video equipment.

There is still no response as the ghostly form remains unmoved and silent.

"Who are you?" asks Rebecca, a second time.

"Well?" asks Mary

The ghostly figure starts to give a response.

"Who I am is of no importance" replies the ghost

"No importance?" asks Kate

"Are you the Gray Lady?" asks Rebecca

The visual scene is of a full-bodied apparition, and they appear to be remarably intelligent.

Peter updates the group.

"Temperature change" advises Peter

"That means more poltergeist activity" replies Rebecca

"Aren't we?" asks Mary

"No were not ... quiet Mary" asks Rebecca

"Are you the Gray Lady" asks Rebecca

"We've met before at Leeds General Infirmary" advises Rebecca

"Do you remember?" asks Mary

"Why didn't you walk into the light?" asks Rebecca

"My work is here" is the ghostly response

"Work?" asks Mary

Peter is continuing to take readings and informs the group.

"We have clear visual readings" advises Peter

Back in York, Nicola and John Paul are now at the Grade Two listed Golden Fleece in the Pavement area of the city.

The Landlord welcomes John Paul and Nicola.

"We have been sent to investigate on behalf of the Police" advises Nicola

"Are you Police?" asks the Landlord

"No, we are investigators of the paranormal" advises John Paul

"Well, you have come to the right place then" advises the Landlord

"Right place?" asks Nicola

"We have had all sorts here … if only these walls could talk, they would" informs the Landlord

The Landlord starts to tell Nicola and John Paul about the traditions of the Golden Fleece and what kind of paranormal activity takes place within its walls.

"We have had Lady Alice Peckett, wife of John Peckett, who used to be the Mayor of York. She wanders about the corridors of the hotel, and is also known as the Gray Lady" advises the Landlord

John Paul and Nicola are amazed at the Landlord's tales.

"We have also had One Eyed Jack and ghosts of Roman soldiers have been seen in the cellar" advises the Landlord

"The Centurian?" asks Nicola

"Who?" asks the Landlord

"We have encountered him before" advises John Paul

"Well, if you are looking to experience ghostly goings on, you have definitely come to the right place. You will certainly find it all here at the Golden Fleece" advises the Landlord

"That's just what DS Mariner told us" advises Nicola

The Golden Fleece Hotel overlooks the Shambles, which is one of York's oldest rows of shops. Its location is close to the Minster.

The Golden Fleece Hotel is a unique building dating back to 1500.

"So, tell us more about Lady Peckett" asks Nicola

"I'll do better than that" replies the Landlord

"I will take you both to where she likes to roam" says the Landlord

John Paul and Nicola follow the Landlord to the upstairs part of the hotel.

"This is where Lady Peckett used to stay" advises the Landlord

The Shambles bedroom has a four-poster double bed, which overlooks the mediaeval street.

John Paul and Nicola start to look around the room for clues.

"So, what are you planning to do?" asks the Landlord

"Probably a late evening vigil" responds John Paul

"Would that be alright?" asks Nicola

"Will the Police also be attending?" asks the Landlord

"No, we are the sole representatives" advises Nicola

"Well, all I can says is happy ghost hunting to the both of you" replies the Landlord

"By the way, Lady Peckett owes me a lot of money" quips the Landlord

"You can be sure we will ask her to pay up" says John Paul

It is now the early hours, and the Golden Fleece Hotel is in complete darkness.

A sudden beam of light fills the corridor, and a ghostly mist appears.

John Paul and Nicola are close by and see an apparition forming.

Suddenly the ghostly vision of The Centurian comes into view.

"You, again" advises Nicola

"Why are you here?" asks John Paul

"Why didn't you walk into the light as instructed?" asks Nicola

"Orders" responds the ghostly figure

"Orders from whom?" asks Nicola

The Centurian offers no response to Nicola's question and stands firm.

Another beam of light appears before them, and the ghostly form of a woman emerges.

"Who are you?" asks Nicola

"Lady Anne Peckett" is the response

"The Gray Lady?" asks John Paul

"Some call me that" responds Lady Peckett

"Who summoned you?" asks Nicola

"The Centurian" replies Lady Peckett

"Are you seeing this, John Paul?" asks Nicola

"Yes, I can see the vision clearly" replies John Paul

"Why are they here?" asks Nicola

The Centurian suddenly retracts back into the ghostly mist with the cohort of soldiers.

Back in Leeds, Rebecca, Mary, Kate, and Peter are continuing their ghost hunt at the Thackray Medical Museum

A ghostly mist appears before them, and a headless spirit appears and challenges the angels.

"Who are you?" asks Rebecca

"Yes, tell us who you are?" asks Mary

"He is the spirit of Piers Galveston, and haunts the 3,000-year-old Scarborough Castle" says Samantha

"If you are who you say you are, why are you here?" asks the ghostly spirit

"What is he talking about?" asks Kate

"He is specifically talking to us" advises Rebecca

"Where are you from?" asks the spirit

Rebecca and Mary reveal their true identities.

Kate and Peter are both frightened.

"Fear not … we are here to help those in distress" advises Mary

"Is it true?" asks Kate

"Yes, it is the truth" advises Rebecca

"The equipment is off the scale again" advises Peter

"Are you tracking this Peter?" asks Kate

"Is it all being recorded?" asks Kate

"Yes, as far as I am aware everything is being recorded" advises Peter

Suddenly, another voice asks a question.

"Do you need our assistance?" asks John Paul

"Where did you come from?" asks Peter

"Nicola and I thought you could do with a helping hand, particularly as both your investigation and the one in York are linked" advises John Paul

"You didn't answer my question, where did you come from" asks Peter

"Lady Peckett and the Gray Lady are both the same person" advises Nicola

Yorkshire is famous for its links to the supernatural World.

The County is a hotbed of paranormal activity with lots of ghost stories which are sure to send a shiver down anyone's spine!

"Do you think we have a problem?" asks John Paul

"Problem?" asks Lady Peckett

"Why does your contrasting form haunt the old workhouse?" asks Nicola

"The Gray Lady is my alter image" replies Lady Peckett

"We are both one in the same" responds Lady Peckett

" and The Centurian?" asks Nicola

"Why?" asks John Paul

"Thank you for helping here at the old workhouse" advises Rebecca

"The old workhouse?" asks Nicola

"Rebecca means Thackray Medical Museum" advises John Paul

"What about the Gray Lady?" asks Nicola

"She has indicated that she and the Gray Lady are one" advises John Paul

A sudden movement takes place indicating more ghostly phenomenon are present.

"What's happening Peter?" asks Kate

"A mirror image" advises Peter

An image of the Gray Lady comes into view on the wall.

"Look it's the Gray Lady" advises Peter

"How strange, we have also been encountering her in York" advises John Paul

"Do you think it is a mirror image?" asks Rebecca

"Well?" asks Nicola

John Paul asks the ghost of Lady Peckett a question.

"Are you a mirror image?" asks John Paul

"I am Lady Alice Peckett. Your Gray Lady is my contrasting image" is the reply

"You are one in the same?" asks John Paul

"She is a visual perception of who I am" informs Lady Peckett

"A visual perception?" asks Nicola

More challenging sightings happen, Peter informs Kate, Mary, and Rebecca of another presence taking shape at the Thackray Medical Museum.

"We have incoming … something else is forming in the mist" advises

Peter

A headless ghost comes forward.

"Who are you?" asks Rebecca

The ghostly figure remains silent.

"The Gray Lady is a disturbance to all those living" advises John Paul

Suddenly, another form enters the ghostly mist.

Dick Turpin on horseback.

"Do you need my help?" asks Turpin

"How can you help?" asks Nicola

"We can summon those who are trapped here" advises Turpin

"We?" asks Nicola

"How?" asks John Paul

"You are the investigators of our fate" responds Turpin

"Let us help you" advises Turpin

"Us?" asks John Paul

The ghostly Centurian reappears with his cohort of Roman soldiers.

PART 3 - HOT OFF THE PRESS

The Press in Leeds and York are in hot pursuit of the real story, and they decide to join forces with the Church in the hope of exposing the Angels.

However, plans to outwit and overthrow them are put into practice. Leeds/York Press Conference with the Managing Editor's prior to the vigil at The Thackray Medical Museum.

At a secret location in Leeds.

"We have recently received new information" advises a reporter

"What have you found out?" asks an Editor

"The information has to do with the pursuit of the angels" advises the reporter

"Is it tangible evidence" asks another Editor

"You may be interested to hear what we have to say" advises the

reporter

"Go on … you've got our attention" advises an Editor

"We have learned that a leading priest at St Anne's Cathedral in Leeds has taken on the role looking for evidence" advises a reporter

"That seems very interesting" advises an Editor

"Do you know the name of the priest in question?" asks an Editor

"All we know is that the Bishop of Leeds has assigned a Monsignor to investigate" advises the Reporter

"Where?" asks an Editor

"If our information is correct, we believe there is a vigil taking place in Leeds and York tonight" advises a reporter

"Where?" asks an Editor

"The Thackray Medical Museum" advises another reporter

"Where did you acquire this information?" asks an Editor

"A very reliable source" advises a reporter

"How very intriguing" advises an Editor

All three Editors start to talk to each other and advise their instructions.

"OK, we all agree that you must check it out, but be discreet" says an Editor

"We intend to go as would be intellectuals" advises a reporter

Nicola and John Paul return to York and continue to challenge the Centurian and Dick Turpin.

"How can you help us?" asks Nicola

"You have a problem concerning the Gray Lady?" asks Turpin

"Centurian" commands John Paul

The Centurian turns but offers no response to that question.

A ghostly cohort of Roman soldier's boots can be heard as they march into view.

"Centurian?" asks Nicola

"Can you help us with the Gray Lady?" asks John Paul

The Centurian is silent then suddenly begins to talk.

"You helped us. We will help you" is the response

"How?" asks John Paul

"We have influence" advises the Centurian

"Influence?" asks Nicola

"He speaks the truth" advises Dick Turpin

"The Gray Lady also lives in York" advises Turpin

"Where you stand" says the Centurian

"Where I stand?" asks Nicola

Suddenly the ghostly form of Lady Alice Peckett now reappears.

Back in Leeds, Rebecca and Mary are taken by surprise by the Gray Lady and the presence of someone else surprises them.

Samantha, the local clairvoyant challenges the Gray Lady.

"I know who you are and why you are here" advises Samantha

"We know of your alter ego" advises Rebecca

"Alter ego?" asks Mary

"Lady Alice Peckett in York" replies Rebecca

There is no response from the Gray Lady.

"How can you be in two places at the same time?" asks Rebecca

Another voice now enters the conversation.

"Yes, answer the lady's question" says the voice

"Why its …" replies Mary

"The Monsignor" replies Rebecca

The Monsignor puts his hand in his pocket and produces a bottle of holy water.

He starts to sprinkle it on the ground.

"I knew there was something different about you two" advises the Monsignor

"You saw the truth" advises Rebecca

"The truth?" asks the Monsignor

"What you saw then and see now is God's work being done" advises Mary

"God's work?" questions the Monsignor

"Who are you?" asks the Monsignor

"We are angels" advises Rebecca

"Why are you pursuing us?" asks Mary

"I have been asked to look for answers" advises the Monsignor

"Answers?" asks Rebecca

"You have found the truth" advises Mary

"Why can't you help us instead of pursuing us?" asks Rebecca

"Help? How can I help you?" asks the Monsignor

"Firstly, by keeping our secret" advises Rebecca

"And secondly?" asks the Monsignor

"By telling no one. You will be our ambassador here on earth" advises Rebecca

"How can I help you?" asks the Monsignor

"By bringing together the Gray Lady and her alternate Lady Alice Peckett" advises Rebecca

"They are both, one in the same person" says Mary

In the background there are two representatives from the press who are secretly filming and making notes.

They think they are safe and unnoticed by the angels.

"We know of your associates" advises Mary

"Associates?" asks the Monsignor

"The gentlemen of the press who are filming and taking notes" advises Rebecca

"I can assure you that they are not with me" informs the Monsignor

"The Gray Lady is an unseen force, yet even I can see her" advises Peter

"Is your equipment recording?" asks the Monsignor

"Yes, but I am not sure exactly what it is recording" advises Peter

The Gray Lady becomes agitated and issues instructions to the Monsignor.

"Stand your ground, priest" advises the ghostly apparition

Samantha now intervenes and offers her help in the stalemate situation.

"Do exactly as she tells you" advises Samantha

"Who are you?" asks the Monsignor

"Samantha is a local clairvoyant, and she is helping us in our investigation" advises Rebecca

The two reporters sneak away into the background.

"Should we be worried about those two?" asks Samantha

"Don't worry" advises Mary

"Their memories and recollections have been erased. They will remember nothing" advises Rebecca

"What about their recording equipment?" asks the Monsignor

"That two has been erased. Their experience has been completely wiped out" advises Rebecca

"How has that been done?" asks the Monsignor

"By divine intervention" advises Rebecca

Back in York, John Paul and Nicola are being asked by Lady Alice Peckett for sanctuary.

"Sanctuary?" asks John Paul

"How can we grant sanctuary" asks Nicola

The ghostly apparition is silent, then begins to respond to their question.

"You can help by bringing my contrasting image in Leeds and my own together" advises the ghost of Lady Alice Peckett

"How?" asks Nicola

"By decree and resolution" advises the apparition

"Can you help me?" asks the ghostly apparition

A sudden brilliant beam of light enters the quaint and traditional room of the public house.

"Peace be with you" advises a voice

"Why it's" says a shocked Nicola

"Michael … welcome" advises John Paul

Michael the Archangel's presence has the Centurian and Dick Turpin's ghosts in fear. Suddenly, the voice of Michael powers over everything.

"Fear not, for I bring you countenance and everlasting peace" advises Michael

"Answers" asks John Paul

"They seek decree and resolution do they not?" asks Michael

"They seek togetherness" advises Nicola

The Monsignor is in awe of Michael and is knelt in adoration.

"Togetherness?" asks Michael

"Can you bring together the worlds of the Gray Lady and Lady Alice Peckett?" asks Nicola

"Yes, all things are possible, by the grace of God" replies Michael

The reporters have now left the investigating area unaware of current events.

They report back to their subsequent Editors, in Leeds and York.

"Well, what have you found out?" asks an Editor

Both reporters check their notebooks only to find all the pages are blank.

"Well?" asks the Editor

"Nothing, absolutely nothing" advises a reporter

"What do you mean nothing?" asks an Editor

"We wrote everything down, but now all the pages are blank" advises a reporter

"How can that have happened?" asks an Editor

"What about video footage?" asks another Editor

Both reporters check their camera phones only to find that nothing has been recorded.

"What's going on?" asks a reporter

"There's nothing on my phone" adds the reporter

"Mine's blank too" advises the other reporter

"Back to the drawing board" advises the Editor

Back at the Shambles room at the Golden Fleece in York, Marie, Peter, Rebecca and Mary have joined Nicola and John Paul.

The illuminated figure of Michael the Archangel stands before them. His brilliant white garment is glowing.

Michael suddenly confirms to all present that the joining of the Gray Lady and Lady Alice Peckett has been completed.

"Let it be known that the Gray Lady also known as Lady Alice Peckett is now at peace in the Kingdom of God" advises Michael

The room is filled with a beam of light and then it falls back into darkness.

The electricity comes back on filling the room once again.

"Michael has left us" advises John Paul

"The Gray Lady and Lady Alice Peckett are now free" advises Samantha

Suddenly, the Police arrive on the scene at the Golden Fleece and at The Thackray Medical Museum in Leeds.

"This way, Sir" advises a young constable

DS Mariner climbs the stairs in the Golden Fleece and enters the Shambles room.

Back in Leeds the late-night vigil at the Thackray Medical Museum has also ended.

"So, what happened?" asks the detective

"We brought together the ghost of the Gray Lady in Leeds and Lady Alice Peckett" advises John Paul

"How, exactly did that happen?" asks the detective

"Both the Gray Lady and Lady Alice Peckett were one in the same" advises Nicola

"Sorry, one in the same ... now you have really lost me" advises the detective

"Lady Alice Peckett and the Gray Lady are both the same person" advises John Paul

"Lady Alice was wandering the corridors here at the Golden Fleece walking up and down the staircases in the dead of night" advises Nicola

"While the Gray Lady was wandering the Leeds General Infirmary and the Thackray Medical Museum" says John Paul

"OK, I think I understand what you are saying" advises the detective

"Case closed?" asks the detective

"Cased closed by decree and resolution" advises John Paul

"By decree?" asks Mariner

"Divine intervention" advises Nicola

Back in Leeds at the Bishop's house a file has been delivered *concerning the angels.*

Could the Angels now need help from Michael the Archangel?

In the Bishop's quarters an aid is summoned.

"Eminence?" asks an aid

"Where is the Monsignor?" asks the Bishop

"At a late-night vigil in the Thackray Museum, Eminence" responds the aid

"Have him report to me immediately on his return" advises the Bishop.

PART 4 - AD INFINITUM

As the Angel's strength grows in Leeds and York their presence is under question and being scrutinised by the Press and Church authorities.

Can they continue, without encountering any problems in today's modern World or will they be forever under suspicion?

Remember, remember the fifth of November?

Guy Fawkes Inn, Petergate, York city centre.

31st October, Halloween. Five days before Bonfire night or as it is widely known Guy Fawkes night.

The historic Inn is the birthplace of Guy Fawkes.

The legendary Catholic born Fawkes began his life in 1570.

He was convicted, aged thirty-five, of high treason after being caught in the middle of a plot to blow up the Houses of Parliament in London.

Guy Fawkes also planned to kill off the King, James the first, and planned to replace him with his nine-year-old daughter, Elizabeth.

The Bar Convent on the outskirts of York.

John Paul, Nicola, and Joseph are in conversation, in a meeting room, about their next investigation.

"So, Joseph, tell us more about Guy Fawkes" asks John Paul

"Guy Fawkes was a Catholic and is still regarded in York as a famous son" advises Joseph

"How does he tie in with our latest investigation?" asks Nicola

"We have been asked to investigate into his ghostly hauntings in York" advises Joseph

"Who has asked for our assistance?" asks John Paul

"The Landlord of the legendary Guy Fawkes Inn" advises Joseph

"Why?" asks Nicola

"The Hotel has been the scene of many hauntings over the years, they have asked us to investigate, as simple as that" advises Joseph

"Who recommended our services?" asks John Paul

"DS Mariner" advises Joseph

"What do you think?" asks John Paul

"It could be a trap" advises Nicola

"What do you think, Joseph?" asks John Paul

"Regardless of what is haunting people there, it does seem to be evident that this lovely little Inn is undeniably very creepy" advises Joseph

"Lovely?" asks John Paul

"The Inn is located within the main historic part of York, yet it is undeniably taboo to many people who think they will not make it through the night" advises Joseph

"Why?" asks Nicola

"In addition to Guy Fawkes, the Landlord advises that the Belfry suite is haunted by two small children who died there" advises Joseph

Back in Leeds, Rebecca, Mary, and Kate are being pursued by the local press and the church.

Intent on finding the truth, Rebecca, Mary, and Kate are invited to Saint Anne's Cathedral by the Bishop.

Park Square meeting room, Rebecca, Mary, and Kate mull over the invitation.

"Well, what do you think?" asks Mary

"An invitation to danger?" responds Kate

"Danger?" asks Rebecca

"Exposure … ad infinitum" advises Mary

"Where's Peter?" asks Mary

"I have sent him ahead as a delegate to the bishop's house" advises Kate

"Why?" asks Rebecca

"Peter will be able to tell what the true meaning is of our invitation … and if we are walking into a trap" advises Kate

"So, it really could be a trap?" asks Mary

"We will soon find out Mary" advises Kate

"What about our next investigation?" asks Rebecca

Kate produces several files and hands them over to Mary and Rebecca.

"Leeds City Varieties" advises Kate

"What is that?" asks Mary

"It's a nineteenth century Music Hall, in the city centre" advises Kate

"Why do they need our help?" asks Rebecca

"The client says the auditorium is a hot bed of paranormal activity" advises Kate

Kate continues to advise Mary and Rebecca about the investigation.

"Poltergeists roam the old-time music venue" advises Kate

"Who is the client?" asks Rebecca

"We have been asked to investigate on behalf of the current owners" advises Kate

"Surely, they knew that inheritance of such phenomena would come with the purchase of the Hall?" asks Mary

A door opens and Peter enters the meeting.

"Good of you to join us" advises Mary

"How did you get on Peter?" asks Kate

"Everything seems to be OK … they are on the level" advises Peter

"On the level?" asks Mary

"Peter means everything has checked out with the Bishop" advises Kate

"Did you discuss the meeting?" asks Rebecca

"I have set a date and time this week for your visit" advises Peter

"When?" asks Rebecca

"Friday at 2pm … is that OK?" asks Peter

"Well, it all depends on our next investigation" advises Rebecca

"OK Kate, contact the owners of the Music Hall and advise them that we will accept the job" advises Rebecca

"It could be a trap" says Peter

"Then you will have to watch out for us Peter" advises Rebecca

"You can always count on me" advises Peter

"We will check in to the City Varieties tomorrow" advises Rebecca

"I agree, inform the owners Kate" says Mary

A spooky encounter awaits in Leeds and in York.

"What about the Bishop's invitation?" asks Kate

"We will make the 2pm meeting on Friday" insists Rebecca

Meanwhile, the press have devised a plan to keep the angels on their toes.

The Guy Fawkes Inn has become synonymous with his birthplace, and it has become well known for his hauntings.

John Paul, Nicola, and Joseph meet the Landlord in the quaint, yet highly toxic atmosphere of the famous York landmark.

The Inn may not be grand, but it is cosy, convenient, and well maintained.

In the snug of the famous Inn, Nicola and John Paul question the Landlord.

"So, how can we help you?" asks John Paul

"Can you perform an exorcism?" asks the Landlord

"An exorcism?" asks Nicola

"Why?" asks Joseph

"I am losing a lot of trade due to ghostly interference" insists the Landlord

"How, exactly?" asks John Paul

"Well, Guy Fawkes is not some wandering lovesick ghost we are talking about here" advises the Landlord

"He really has many issues" says the Landlord

"He's a ghost" advises John Paul

"What kind of issues?" asks Nicola

"Somehow, he is committed to his cause" advises the Landlord

"His cause?" asks Nicola

"We are only a few days away from Bonfire night" advises the Landlord

"Bonfire night?" asks John Paul

"Guy Fawkes was discovered that night, trying to blow up the Houses of Parliament in London … and he also had a very gruesome death" advises the Landlord

"How, exactly?" asks Nicola

The Landlord continues to tell his story about Guy Fawkes.

"Guy Fawkes was tortured, and he ultimately died by hanging" advises the Landlord

"So, why do you need the exorcism?" asks John Paul

"Guy Fawkes masquerades as a poltergeist here in York" advises the Landlord

"But isn't that a good thing?" asks Joseph

"A good thing?" asks Nicola

"People from all over the World come to your Inn?" advises Joseph

"Without the ghost of Guy Fawkes there would be no tourism for you" advises Joseph

"I had not really thought about that" advises the Landlord

John Paul steps in to advise they will take on the investigation.

"OK, we will help" advises John Paul

"We will see what we can do" advises Nicola

The Landlord now is in two minds as to whether he should go ahead with the exorcism or not.

Back in Leeds, Rebecca, Mary, Kate, and Peter are now at the famous City Varieties Musica Hall in the city centre.

They are in conversation with the owner of the City Varieties.

"Do you believe in ghosts?" asks the owner

"Naturally, we believe in their existence" advises Nicola

"Where are my manners … my name is Bill Atherton. I am the current owner of the Music Hall" advises Bill

Rebecca makes the introductions and assures the owner of their help.

Peter steps in with another take on the paranormal activity at the venue.

"I am a bit sceptical" advises Peter

"What about you?" asks the owner

"I believe they do exist" advises Mary

"How can we help you?" asks Rebecca

"I believe, you are investigators of the paranormal?" asks the owner

"Yes, amongst other things" advises Rebecca

Bill Atherton takes the Angel's Eyes Investigations team on a tour of the famous Music Hall, starting in the main auditorium.

"Are you all feeling brave?" asks the owner

"Brave?" asks Kate

"You will need to be, to go any further" advises the owner

"You've got our attention Bill" advises Peter

"Please tell us … what exactly are we up against?" asks Rebecca

"Things that just don't add up, or do they?" advises the owner

"In what way?" asks Rebecca

"Surely you knew that such a venue as this would be haunted when you decided to buy the building?" asks Peter

"A lot of famous people have performed here" advises the owner

"Who, exactly?" asks Mary

"Charlie Chaplin and Harry Houdini to mention just two of the acts" advises the owner

Mary decides to step in and offers her take on the investigation.

"OK, Bill … where do we start?" asks Mary

Meanwhile outside of the City Varieties several newspaper reporters have gathered looking for a story.

Rebecca and Mary decide to change their identities to deal with the Investigation due to the complicated chain of events.

Kate and Peter have been dispatched by Rebecca and Mary to look for the existence of ghostly phenomena in the auditorium.

Rebecca and Mary return to the auditorium, disguised as stage performers.

"I know I left it here somewhere" says Maggie aka Mary

"Girls" asks the owner

"Why are you both here?" asks the owner

"Would you believe it … we've lost our mojo" replies Ruth aka Rebecca

"Your mojo?" laughs the owner

"Is this a joke?" asks the owner

Both girls and the owner begin to laugh on stage, then suddenly hear a very loud bang.

Meanwhile, a shadowy presence in the wings of the old time Music Hall emerges into view in a cloudy mist.

"Did you hear that?" asks the owner

"What?" asks Kate

Maggie and Ruth join the owner on stage, in the auditorium.

"What's all the fuss about?" asks Maggie

"Another stage prank?" asks Ruth

"Was it a ghost?" asks the owner

"I will check my recording equipment" advises Peter

Back in York, Nicola and John Paul begin to summon the ghost of Guy Fawkes.

A bright light and ghostly mist appear in the basement of the Inn and a figure begins to emerge from the shadows.

John Paul starts to alure the figure to appear before them.

"Who are you?" asks John Paul

The ghostly figure offers no response to John Paul's question.

Nicola asks the question a second time.

"Who are you?" asks Nicola

"Are you Guy Fawkes?" asks John Paul

"I am he" responds the ghostly figure

"Why do you haunt this place?" asks Nicola

"This is my birthplace" advises the ghostly figure

"But you are dead" advises John Paul

"Why do you seek the dead among the living?" asks Nicola

The ghost of Guy Fawkes offers no response and remains silent and rigid.

"You are only halfway between" advises John Paul

"Between Heaven and Earth" says Nicola

"Halfway?" responds the ghostly figure

"Why?" questions the ghostly figure

"You need to walk back into the light" advises John Paul

"The light?" asks the ghostly figure

"You should have walked into the light" advises Nicola

"How?" asks the ghostly figure

Joseph suddenly decides to help. John Paul and Nicola rectify the situation.

"Let me help" advises Joseph

"OK, Joseph" advises John Paul

Joseph addresses the ghost directly and tries to put his point forward.

"You are Guy Fawkes … you are in York not London" advises Joseph

"London?" asks the ghostly figure

"The place of your crime" advises Joseph

"Crime?" asks the ghostly figure

John Paul and Nicola begin to perform an exorcism.

The Landlord rushes in to stop the exorcism being performed.

"I have decided not to go ahead with the exorcism" advises the Landlord

"So, you welcome the ghost of Guy Fawkes?" asks Nicola

"Yes, he is part of the building … and without him I would be ruined" advises the Landlord

John Paul and Nicola agree to stop the exorcism.

Back in Leeds, Rebecca, and Mary, now disguised as stage performers, Ruth and Maggie, agree to help the current owner of the City Varieties.

"Do you want us to perform an exorcism?" asks Maggie

"I thought you were both stage performers?" asks the owner

"We are ladies of many talents" advises Ruth

"The theatre is alive" advises Maggie

"It has a soul" advises Ruth

As they perform an exorcism, the press flood into the auditorium but only find Kate and Peter with the owner.

Maggie and Ruth aka Mary and Rebecca have left the auditorium.

"We've been left holding the baby" advises Peter

"Not necessarily" advises the owner

"What does he mean?" asks Kate

"What happened to Maggie and Ruth?" asks Peter

"Where are Rebecca and Mary" asks Kate

LUCKY, LUCKY ME

In the dramatic finale, Brian attempts to take his life again. The angels must deal with illusions and blurred vision. A double decker bus turns over in the centre of Leeds. The angels masquerade as Emergency Service staff … reports

of a heavenly glow. We are here to serve you. The Press begin the look for answers and start hounding the angels … The final revelation and disappearance …

The Bar Convent, York … John Paul and Nicola are in conversation in one of the meeting rooms …

"Do you remember Brian and Lendal Bridge?" asks John Paul

"Yes, I remember" says Nicola

"He is attempting to commit suicide again at the top of the Woodhouse Car Park near to the Infirmary in Leeds" advises John Paul

"We must get in touch with Rebecca and Mary" says Nicola

Joseph walks into the meeting and advises that he will contact Kate to advise her of the potential suicide …

Joseph uses his mobile and Kate's phone begins to ring …

"Hi Kate … it's Joseph" says the voice

"Hello Joseph" responds Kate

"We had a case, a gentleman called Brian … he almost took his life on Lendal Bridge in York, but luckily John Paul and Nicola managed to persuade him to change his mind" advises Joseph

"Have there been any other developments?" asks Kate

"Well, yes there has … now he is trying to do it again … can you help?" asks Joseph

"Where exactly do you want us to go?" asks Kate

"We believe that he is attempting to jump off the Woodhouse car park roof" advises Joseph

"How do you know that?" asks Kate

"Tell her intuition … divine countenance" says John Paul

Joseph relays the message to Kate …

"Divine countenance?" advises Joseph

"OK … Rebecca and Mary say they will investigate … we will be in touch" advises Kate

Joseph advises John Paul and Nicola …

Mary, Rebecca, and Kate arrive on the top floor of the Woodhouse car park, near the Merrion Centre, where a crowd is beginning to gather …

"Don't jump mate, nothing is worth jumping for" shouts someone in the crowd

"Sound advice" says another

"Leave me alone … leave me alone" advises Brian

Rebecca decides to call up to Brian …

"Brian?" asks Rebecca

"Who are you?" asks Brian

"I am Rebecca, this is Mary, we are associates of John Paul and Nicola" advises Rebecca

"I will only speak to John Paul , no one else" advises Brian

"OK Brian, we understand … we will ask John Paul to get here as soon as possible" responds Rebecca

Being an angel … John Paul arrives on the scene in an instant …

"Where did you come from?" asks Kate

"I was already on my way … somehow I thought you might need my help" advises John Paul

John Paul calls up to Brian … "Why are you up there Brian?"

"John Paul, you have arrived … I will speak only to you" insists Brian

"OK I am here … now what is all this about Brian?" asks John Paul

"I am coming up Brian" says John Paul

"Don't try anything, OK?" advises Brian

"I understand" says John Paul

John Paul heads up to the top of the roof to find Brian near the edge.

"What's this all about Brian?" asks John Paul

"I thought we had sorted all of this out at Lendal Bridge … what happened?" asks John Paul

"It feels like they are pulling the four walls down on top of me" advises Brian

"Why does it feel that way Brian?" asks John Paul

"I am not strong enough to stop them" replies Brian

"Who?" asks John Paul

"I am blind, and I cannot see" says Brian

"Only your vision is blurred Brian … let me be your eyes" advises John Paul

"Please can you help him?" asks a lady

"Who are you?" asks Nicola

"I am Pamela, I am his wife" replies the lady

"We will do our best" says Nicola

"You see he has been suffering from depression for many years … we fear it is the end this time" says Pamela

"Do you believe, Brian?" asks John Paul

"Yes, I believe … but I still haven't found what I am looking for" replies Brian

"What are you searching for Brian?" asks John Paul

Suddenly, Brian loses a footing and the crowd gasps …

"Are you alright Brian?" asks John Paul

"I am alright, but next time …" replies Brian

"So, what do you really want Brian?" asks John Paul

"I have everything, yet I am not satisfied … life has let me down" says Brian

"Hold on Brian" advises John Paul

Meanwhile, Rebecca and Mary have another emergency to attend to in the City Centre where a double decker bus has overturned …

"We must leave Nicola" advises Mary

"Tell John Paul we will return as soon as possible" advises Rebecca

The overturned double decker bus is a new all electric hybrid, which is Hydrogen powered … it was full at the time of the accident.

Mary and Rebecca are now at the scene on the Headrow …

"Quick, Mary, Rebecca … a bus has overturned in the city centre, can you help?" asks Kate

"We must get there soon, before it's too late" advises Rebecca

Mary and Rebecca are at the scene in an instant …

"What happened?" asks Mary

"A car shot across the path of the bus, and it had to swerve, then it turned over on to its side" advises a witness

"Have the emergency services been notified?" asks Rebecca

"They are on their way" says another witness

"OK, we must act quickly" advises Rebecca

"Be careful when you go inside" advises Kate

"Thank you … we will" says Rebecca

On entry several passengers are needing urgent medical attention and some of them have passed out …

Suddenly a voice cries out … "Help me, please help me"

"What's your name?" asks Mary

"Tina … my name is Tina" responds the voice

"OK Tina … where does it hurt?" asks Rebecca

"All over … I am in so much pain" responds Tina

"Take my hand" advises Rebecca

"What's happening?" asks Tina

A radiant glow starts to radiate from Rebecca …

"It's a new kind of medicine" advises Rebecca

"How do you feel now?" asks Mary

"Much better … as if it never happened" responds Tina

"OK … who is next?" asks Mary

"Well, there are two over here" says a voice

"OK, we have come to help" says Mary

"How do you do it?" asks a voice

"Oh, it's a secret … we can't tell you at the moment" responds Rebecca

"Mary, can you assist?" asks Rebecca

"What do you want me to do Rebecca?" asks Mary

"If you could help with these two passengers" asks Rebecca

"Hold on" says Mary

A beam of bright light falls on to the passengers ...

"How do you feel now?" asks Mary

"Wonderful" is the response

"Who are you?" asks a passenger

"We are part of the Emergency Services" replies Rebecca

"Now we must find those who are not responding" advises Mary

"OK Mary, we need to make a big effort this time" says Rebecca

Another beam of light appears ...

All are responding and coming round ...

"How can we all thank you?" asks Tina

"Just live good lives" advises Mary

"We all promise" say the passengers

"Our colleagues are on their way" advises Rebecca

Mary and Rebecca disappear from the scene ...

Paramedics and Emergency ambulances arrive on the scene with all lights flashing and all sirens wailing ...

"OK ... who needs urgent attention?" asks a paramedic

"No one ... your colleagues have already sorted us out" says a passenger

"Who ... how?" asks a nurse

When the passengers describe Mary and Rebecca, they are startled ...

"We know of no such colleagues" advises a doctor

"A beam of light saved us ... they told us it was a new kind of medicine" advises Tina

"What beam of light?" replies a doctor

"There is no medicine like that" insists the doctor

"Angels ... they were angels" advises a young man

"They saved all our lives" say the passengers

"Praise be God" say the passengers

News of the overturned double decker in Leeds is now national news and reporters from all over the World are marvelling at the way the victims and passengers were saved by two strangers and a radiant beam of light …

Meanwhile, Brian is still on the Woodhouse car park roof, and he is threating to take his life …

"I'll do it … come no nearer … that's near enough" advises Brian

John Paul is now assisted by Nicola, who has brought Brian's wife Pamela on to the roof top in hope that she may be able to coax him down …

"They can take my life, but they can't take my pride" advises Brian

"No one wants to hurt you Brian" replies John Paul

"Come down, Brian" asks Pamela

"I don't want to live without you" advises Pamela

"Love is not an easy thing, Pamela" replies Brian

"I have always done my best" insists Brian

"… but it's time to go" says Brian

"No, Brian … we're here to save you" replies John Paul

"We saved you last time … listen to John Paul" advises Nicola

"What you have … no one can take away from you" replies John Paul

"I don't have anything" responds Brian

"You have everything … let us help you" adds Nicola

"We helped you before, let us help you again" says John Paul

"Take one more step and I will do it" advises Brian

Nicola and John Paul decide to try another tactic with Brian's wife approval …

"I only want to bring you a cup of tea" advises John Paul

"Cup of tea?" asks Brian

"OK ... leave it there" advises Brian

"I am going where no one can follow" insists Brian

"Don't do it Brian" asks Nicola

... but with one last farewell Brian jumps to his death ...

Pamela screams and the crowd gathered round are in total shock ...

"We failed him" advises Nicola

"No one could have helped" replies John Paul

"Brian had made up his mind" advises John Paul

"Maybe if we lay our hands on him" says Nicola

"I believe it is too late Nicola ... way too late" says John Paul

"I'm sorry" says Nicola

News of Brian jumping off the Woodhouse car park roof reaches the press, and they are hot on the heels of John Paul, Nicola, Mary, and Rebecca ...

The Press turn up at the Park Square office suite and they encounter something unusual ...

"Yes, how can I help you?" asks Kate

"We've come to see John Paul, Nicola, Mary and Rebecca" says a reporter

"Who?" asks Kate

"Sorry you must be mistaken" insists Kate

"This is the Angel's Eyes Investigations office, isn't it?" asks the reporter

"The Angel's agency?" asks another reporter

"Sorry, there is no such organisation here ... you must have got the wrong address" advises Kate

"What do they want" says another voice

"They are asking about an Angel's Investigations Agency" replies Kate

"My name is Stephen O'Hare. I am a barrister of these chambers" *replies the voice*

"We have never heard of it, sorry but there is no such office here" *advises the barrister*

The reporters are shocked at their response and leave the offices.

The real Angel's have left, never to be seen again?

Who knows for ... GOD WORKS IN MYSTERIOUS WAYS HIS WONDERS TO PERFORM ...

As for the Angels, their work is never done ... they watch over all of us for all time ... for all Eternity.

CHRISTMAS ANGELS

The famous Christmas Angels shop in Low Petergate, York, was an all year round seller and provider of Christmas ornaments situated in the very heart of the bustling shopping centre near the Minster ...

When the lease on the grade 2 listed property came up no one came forward to use the premises for alternative use ...

This seasonal set of stories reunites John Paul, Rebecca, Mary, and Nicola.

The Angel's are reassigned by Michael the Archangel and assume the roles of Proprietors of the famous Christmas Angels shop on a short-term lease with a view to permanency.

The Angels are shopkeepers with a difference, and they become engaged in various angelic and human situations all with a magical Christmas feeling.

The stories take in various locations in York.

Will the angels be found out or will their true identities remain an angelic secret?

ON THE FIRST DAY OF CHRISTMAS

... AN ANGEL CAME TO ME

In the realms of Heaven ...

Michael the Archangel has summoned Angel's Rebecca and Mary ...

"Rebecca and Mary ... I have another challenge for you" advises Michael

"May we ask Michael what that challenge is?" asks Rebecca

"I am assigning you both to the aptly named Christmas Angels shop in York" advises Michael

"York?" asks Mary

"Wouldn't Nicola and John Paul be more capable as they were previously at The Bar Convent there?" asks Rebecca

"They will assist you" advises Michael

"You see, we are coming too" advises John Paul

"Yes, we will all work together there" advises Nicola

"What is the assignment, Michael?" asks Rebecca

"It has come to our attention that the Christmas Angels shop has now closed. You will take over it, as they say, on a short-term lease" advises Michael

"There will also be an option for permanency" advises Michael

"It's the perfect cover ... no one will suspect you" insists Michael

The shop used to specialise in the sale of Christmas decorations on an all year round basis.

"The original proprietors have decided to retire leaving the shop empty" advises Michael

"You will also benefit from the additional live in accommodation" confirms Michael

"We have a provisional set of assignments for you to deal with" advises Michael

"May we ask what they are all about?" asks Mary

"All in good time, Mary ... all in good time" responds Michael

"We can use it to the best of our ability" replies Michael

"You will be shopkeepers with difference" advises Michael

"You can familiarise yourselves. You will have Kate and Peter as your assistants" advises Michael

"Are you OK with that, Nicola?" asks John Paul

"Yes, of course" advises Nicola

"They too have been assigned" advises Michael

"Do they know?" asks John Paul

"No, they don't know yet, but we will deal with that as required" advises Michael

"When do we start?" asks Rebecca

"Immediately" replies Michael

A bright light illuminates the room ... and in an instant John Paul, Nicola, Rebecca, and Mary arrive in Lower Petergate, York, outside of the Christmas Angel's shop ...

The large front windows are stacked with toys and dolls house furniture with teddy bears all over the place ... Inside it is a children's adventure playground ...

Mary is taken aback with all the toys on offer ...

"Oh, it's a wonderful shop" advises Mary

"Look at all those toys" says Nicola

"Michael was right ... this is the perfect cover" advises Rebecca

"Can you believe it ... real angel's running a shop called Christmas Angels in York?" replies Nicola

"It's a dream come true" advises Mary

"No one will suspect" advises John Paul

"Remember what Michael said" advises John Paul

"I remember … it is a short-term lease, but it may become permanent" replies Rebecca

"Look, there is also a Noel Christmas shop a few doors away … maybe we can gain some experience from them?" asks Mary

"We need to get our bearings first" advises John Paul

"Remember, why Michael sent us here" replies Rebecca

"We are in an outstanding position; we are close to the Minster and the heart of the city" advises Nicola

"We need to get a feeling of where we are Mary" replies John Paul

The Angels decide to take a walk into the city, where they find a Christmas market with lots of tourists and bargain hunters …

It's Yorks' fiftieth year of the Saint Nicholas Fair. There are over a hundred stalls in the very narrow cobbled streets which are surrounded by wonky buildings. Christmas music is being played and there is a lot of festive entertainment along the way …

The market is horrendously busy with lots of people looking for Christmas gifts …

Close to the Christmas Angels shop a huge part of the market is in full swing and lots of tourists are waiting for the Christmas lights to be switched on …

"Maybe I can help you?" asks a voice

"Nicola" says a surprised Rebecca

"Where did you come from?" asks John Paul

"I thought I would check out the market ahead of you all" advises Nicola

"What did you find, Nicola?" asks Mary

"Just lots of people enjoying themselves, it really is a wonderful atmosphere" advises Nicola

It is now almost switch on time for the Christmas lights. The mayor makes an announcement …

He climbs on to the makeshift stage ...

"OK everyone ... you need to be ready when we launch the countdown" advises the mayor

"Are you all ready?" asks the mayor

Everyone shouts in a loud voice and the crowd become excited ...

Suddenly, the crowd surges forward to the front and tragically a young girl is crushed in the rush ...

The young girl's life hangs in the balance ...

"Help ... can anyone help me" cries a young woman

"How can we help you?" asks John Paul

"My little girl, Maria, has been crushed in the crowd surge ... can you help me?" asks the young girl's mother

Someone in the crowd phones for the paramedics and an emergency ambulance ...

"We will help you ... what is your name?" asks Nicola

"My name is Sandy" says the young mother

"OK Sandy ... I am Nicola ... this is Rebecca and Mary" reply the angels

"Why is she breathing?" asks Sandy

"Lay her down and we will try to revive her" advises Rebecca

Sandy lays Maria down on the road ...

"Are you nurses?" asks Sandy

"Yes ... of a kind" replies Nicola

Mary, Rebecca, and Nicola administer the laying of hands-on Maria ... and a white radiant beam of light appears ...

Everyone in the crowd looks around in astonishment ...

"What's happening?" asks Sandy

"It's a new type of medicine" advises Mary

"A magic formula?" asks Sandy

"Yes … exactly" replies Nicola

"Who are you?" asks Sandy

The young girl responds and is soon sitting up awake …

"What happened to me?" asks Maria

The large crowd gather round …

"If these ladies hadn't helped me …" replies Maria

"What ladies?" asks someone in the crowd

"There's no one here" says another voice in the crowd

"Except for this" advises another passer by

A mound of white feathers on the ground …

"It's a miracle" shouts Sandy

"A Christmas miracle" says someone in the crowd

"My daughter was unconscious … fighting for her life, now she lives" replies Sandy

"I must thank them" insists Sandy

"They were real angels" says Sandy

"The spirit of Christmas is alive" says someone in the crowd

"It's all real" replies Sandy

"My baby has been saved by Angels" shouts Sandy

News quickly spreads to the media of a miraculous recovery in York.

The spirit of Christmas has saved a young girl's life.

The Editor at the York Press issues orders to his reporters …

"We must send our specialised reporters to look into this as soon as possible" advises the Editor

News also reaches the Bar Convent of the miraculous lifesaving phenomenon.

"We must make haste" advises Nicola

"We can take refuge in the Bar Convent" replies John Paul

Mary, Rebecca, and Nicola arrive at the Convent ...

On arrival they are met by Peter who is extremely happy to see Nicola again.

"You have come back to me, Nicola" says Peter

"You see, when I said for all Eternity ... that's exactly what I meant" advises Nicola

"You know Mary and Rebecca, don't you?" asks Nicola

"Yes of course ... I am so happy to see all of you" replies Peter

"When did you arrive back in York?" asks Peter

"We have just taken over the Christmas Angels shop in Low Petergate initially for the Christmas season ... but if we are successful, we may be there permanently" advises Nicola

"Successful?" asks Peter

"Oh, the original owners may be a hard act to follow, but we will try to implement our own special formula" advises Rebecca

"Yes, it is a wonderful shop" advises Mary

"I have recently spoken to Kate in Leeds" advises Peter

"How is she?" asks Rebecca

"Is she happy?" asks Mary

"Well, yes I believe she is well and happy too" replies Peter

"Kate has agreed to join us in running Christmas Angels" advises Peter

"Now, about this formula" asks Peter

"Is it a magic formula?" asks Peter

"Magic?" asks Nicola

"Why do you ask?" replies Mary

"Well, I may have a surprise for you all" replies Peter

In walks John Paul ...

"I can see I have taken you all by surprise" says John Paul

"Where have you been?" asks Rebecca

"While you were watching the Christmas switch on, I was looking into Christmas Angels ..." advises John Paul

"You will make a good shop keeper, John Paul" responds Nicola

"I am the Proprietor" advises John Paul

"We all are" replies Mary

"At least we will have you to watch over us now" says Nicola

"That is the very least I will do" advises John Paul

ON THE SECOND DAY
OF CHRISTMAS

... THE GIFT OF LOVE CAME TO ME

It's Christmas Eve in York and Kate, Peter, Rebecca, and Mary are remarkably busy in the Christmas Angels shop in Low Petergate.

Nicola and John Paul are attending another event, across the city ...

Kate is certainly in the Christmas spirit ...

"It's getting so exciting" advises Kate

"Well, it is Christmas Eve, Kate" replies Peter

Mary and Rebecca are mingling with the customers in the background ...

"May I purchase this exquisite glass angel, please?" asks a customer

"Yes, of course ... an excellent choice" advises Rebecca

"One of our finest" responds Mary

"I am so glad that you have taken over Christmas Angels" says the customer

"Oh, we are only too pleased to help, and be of assistance" replies Kate

"It has got quite a reputation" advises the customer

"Thank you so much for your kind words" replies Rebecca

"Have a nice day" says the customer

"Merry Christmas" replies the customer

"Happy Christmas to you too" responds Rebecca

The distinguished customer leaves the shop and walks towards the Minster ...

"You know who that was don't you?" asks Kate

"No ... who?" asks Rebecca

"The Dean of York Minster" advises Kate

"The Dean?" asks Rebecca

"Well, I never" says Mary

"Does the Pope ever call in?" asks Mary

"Only on his off days" laughs Peter

"Really, Peter?" asks Rebecca

"No ... I am sorry he doesn't!" replies Kate

"Sorry, that was a joke ... you know as in sense of humour" advises Peter

Across York, at the Knavesmire lies York Racecourse, Nicola, and

John Paul are attending a Christmas Eve Ball, all in good faith of course.

A private celebration is taking place in the main suite, and it is rammed packed with Christmas revellers who are all in the festive spirit …

A top-quality catering and hospitality team are on standby to make the occasion an outstanding success …

"Who invited us to the event, John Paul?" asks Nicola

"While you, Rebecca and Mary were at the Christmas Light switch on I was talking with several dignitaries of York and they offered me several tickets … well two to be exact … that is why we are here" advises John Paul

"Well, it certainly has a Christmas Eve feel to it" replies Nicola

"The Christmas spirit is truly well and alive" advises John Paul

Another voice greets them to the special evening …

"May I have your invitations, please" says the voice

John Paul hands over the tickets …

"Ah, you're both from Christmas Angels in the city" asks the greeter

"Welcome, your table is B5" advises the greeter

"I will show you to your table" replies a waiter

"Thank you" replies Nicola

Several people are already seated at the table …

"This is Steve Hunt … he is from Noel also in York" advises the waiter

"Good evening to you both" advises John Paul

"My name is Steve … this is my partner Sarah" replies Steve

"Hello, I am John Paul … this is my associate, Nicola" advises John Paul

"You're both new to the city, aren't you?" asks Steve

"We've just taken over Christmas Angels" advises Nicola

"Rivals?" asks Steve

"We hope not" replies John Paul

"More like ... watching over things" replies Nicola

"If you know what we mean" advises John Paul

"We're not in competition with anyone" advises Nicola

"Excellent, I think we're all going to be good friends" replies Steve

"So do we" advises John Paul

The evening gets underway with a five course Christmas banquet, followed by various speeches from owners of shops and stores in the city ... then the Christmas festivities begin ...

"Are you both married?" asks Steve

"Oh, no ... we're married to what we do" advises Nicola

"Ah, I understand clearly now" says Steve

"We're basically entrepeneur's on a journey through time" advises John Paul

"Time?" asks Sarah

"All time" advises Nicola

The DJ announces that the party is about to commence ...

"I have to advise you that strobe lighting will be in use tonight" advises the DJ

The first Christmas record begins to play ... everyone starts to go on the dance floor ...

"Fancy a boogie?" asks Sarah

"A boogie?" replies Nicola

"Oh, she means a dance, Nicola" advises John Paul

"Well, I ..." responds Nicola

"Go on Nicola ... you know how you love to dance" advises John Paul

"I do?" asks Nicola

"Well, I will do my best" advises Nicola

It's not long before the dance floor is filled with Christmas revellers …

Suddenly, a situation, unexpectedly alters the festivities …

At a table nearby, someone is in difficulty …

"Derek, are you alright?" asks his wife

"I don't know, Teresa … I feel so different" advises Derek

"Perhaps we should sit down" replies Teresa

Derek has no longer sat down when he suffers a heart attack …

"Oh, my God … please someone help me, quick" asks Teresa

Nicola is first on the scene followed by John Paul … Sarah and Steve …

"Can you hear me?" asks Nicola

There is no response from Derek …

"What's his name?" asks Nicola

"Derek" replies Teresa

"I'm his wife" replies Teresa

"I think he is having a heart attack" advises John Paul

"Do you have a defibrillator here?" asks Nicola

"We'll try and locate one" advises Steve

Nicola and John Paul realise their cover may be blown and leave the scene for a few minutes and change their identities …

John Paul and Nicola return as doctor and nurse.

Suddenly Derek starts to respond …

"I can hear angelic music, harps playing and the smell of sweet biscuits and chocolate" advises Derek

"He is delirious" advises Teresa

"Quick … he is near" responds the nurse aka Nicola

"Near?" asks Teresa

"Yes ... passing from this World into the next" says Nicola

"How do you know?" asks Teresa

"Oh, I have read about it ... I am a nurse" advises Nicola

"We will have to administer the laying of hands, before it's too late" says the doctor aka John Paul

"John Paul, join me, we may just be in time" asks Nicola

They join hands and a bright beam of light radiates from them both ...

"What is happening?" asks Teresa

"The Christmas spirit is now descending on Derek ... he will live" advises John Paul

Christmas revellers at the function now start to gather round ...

"How can I thank you?" asks Teresa

"Give thanks to God for Derek's life and tell no one what has happened here tonight" advises Nicola

"But all these people saw it happen" replies Teresa

"You won't remember anything when we are gone" says John Paul

"All you will remember is that Derek made it" advises Nicola

"Who are you?" asks Teresa

"We are angels ... we only administer and appear on rare occasions ... tonight it was to save Derek" advises John Paul

"Tell him what we have done for him ... and to live a long life" advises Nicola

"He deserves a second chance" advises John Paul

"Now we must leave you" says Nicola

"I know who you are" says someone in the crowd

"You will only remember that Derek was saved and is alive ... that is all you will know when we are gone" says John Paul

"Please don't follow where we are going" advises Nicola

"What you see before you is an illusion ... you see us as two people" advises John Paul

"Those people do not exist ... our images have been created for us to carry out our work" advises Nicola

"Where are you going?" asks Teresa

"Back to Our Lord and Master" advises John Paul

"You mean ..." asks Teresa

"Yes, the very same" advises Nicola

"If we meet again, it will be on the other side" advises John Paul

"Now, we must go" advises John Paul

They both leave the scene ...

The two created images and identities change back into Nicola and John Paul ...

Steve and Sarah return with the defibrillator ...

"Where's Derek?" asks Steve

"I'm here" advises Derek

"But you're alright?" replies Sarah

"What happened?" asks Sarah

Nicola and John Paul return as themselves and no one is more the wiser ...

"Where have you been?" asks Teresa

"What happened?" asks Nicola

"You have missed it all" advises Sarah

"Yes, where were you?" asks Steve

"Oh, we found another defibrillator on the course" advises Nicola

"Are we too late" asks John Paul

"No, on the contrary ... Derek is alright, his life has been saved"

advises Teresa

"Saved by whom?" asks John Paul

"We don't really know" advises Teresa

"All I can remember is that Derek is alive and well" says Teresa

"Well, that's a good enough celebration for anything" says Nicola

"The miracle of Christmas is still very much alive" advises John Paul

"A miracle" advises Teresa

"Miracle?" asks John Paul

"Angels" replies Teresa

"Was it the Archangel Gabriel?" asks Nicola

"I don't know" advises Derek

"It was the gift of Love on Christmas Eve" advises John Paul

ON THE THIRD DAY OF CHRISTMAS

... THE GHOST OF CHRISTMAS
PAST CAME TO ME

It is now Boxing Day or Saint Stephen's Day, and Peter has invited Rebecca, Mary, Nicola, and John Paul to go with him on a Ghost walk in York ...

CHRISTMAS ANGELS SHOP IN LOW PETERGATE, YORK CITY CENTRE ...

The bells are being rung at the Minster ...

John Paul is in conversation with Peter ...

"You do know today is actually Saint Stephen's day don't you, Peter?" asks John Paul

"Yes, happy Saint Stephen's day, John Paul" replies Peter

"We enjoyed Christmas ... what have you got in mind today?" asks Nicola

"It's also known as Boxing Day" advises Peter

"Yes, but did you know that the real Christmas is actually 11/09/3BC?" asks John Paul

"No ... I didn't!" replies Peter

"The Christmas everyone celebrates on the 25th of December was adapted to coincide with the Winter Solstice" advises John Paul

"So, Peter, do you have any suggestions today?" asks Nicola

"I thought we would all go on a ghost walk of our ancient city" replies Peter

"What do you think?" asks John Paul

"I think that's a splendid idea" advises Rebecca

"What have you got in mind?" asks Nicola

"Well, if we all meet in the Shambles for 7.30pm tonight ... all will be revealed" advises Peter

The Ghost walk is a unique opportunity to discover the hidden magic of the ancient city of York, which is told through the real art of storytelling. Tales are drawn from the history of York and are revealed with a backdrop of haunting beauty.

Later that evening in The Shambles, centre of York ...

A guide shouts out his instructions to everyone ... there is about 25 gathered together for the tour ...

The guide begins his rendition by laying out some facts about the walk ...

"The genuine ... see the authentic ... the magical ... the incredibly famous ... all will be revealed on our tour of the city ..." advises the guide

"Ghost hunters and ghouls follow me through the streets of York ... everything will be revealed" says the guide

By now an even bigger group has congregated in the wake of the guide ...

"It all sounds very intriguing" advises Mary

"Be prepared for our journey will take all your emotions on a ride of horror and it will tantalise the excitement inside you" advises the guide

"Very dramatic, isn't he?" replies Rebecca

As they walk through York's magnificent architecture, maze of streets and snickets the tour begins ...

The group suddenly come to a halt ...

"My name is Mark. I am your guide for the evening" says the guide

"Welcome to York everyone" advises Mark

"Now, I have a spooky tale to tell you ..." advises Mark

Just as Mark starts to begin his pitch, another phenomenon begins to take place …

"Did you see that?" asks Mary

"No, what did you see Mary?" asks Rebecca

"A ghostly sighting" advises Mary

"Was it real?" asks John Paul

"Can you see it, Peter?" asks Nicola

"Yes … and it's coming straight towards us" advises Peter

No one else in the group can see the apparition except for the Angels and Peter …

The apparition summons the Angels …

"Do you remember me?" asks the apparition

"Who are you?" asks John Paul

"I am the ghost of Christmas Past" says the apparition

"What do you want?" asks Rebecca

"I want to be freed and to go forward" replies the ghost

"How can we free you?" asks Nicola

"Roman soldiers live here, and they are marching down the road" says the apparition

"We can see no one" advises John Paul

"They are walking on their knees" replies the ghost

"On their knees?" asks Mary

"They are looking for a roman road" advises the apparition

"But where does it go?" asks Peter

"No where … they came out of a wall" replies the ghost

"Out of a wall … I don't understand" advises Peter

"I have heard them talking but I can't understand what they are saying" says the ghost

"Are they talking in another language?" asks Nicola

"If they are Roman soldiers they will be talking in Italian" advises John Paul

"They all chant the name of Caesar" advises the ghost

"They are marching towards the Minster" advises the apparition

"Can you help me?" asks the ghost

"We will try?" advises Rebecca

"We must head them off before they reach the Minster" says the apparition

The Roman soldiers head towards the Minster but the Angels appear ahead of them ...

"In the name of Caesar, you are ordered to halt" shouts John Paul

"Who are you?" asks the Centurian

"We are the guardians of York" advises John Paul

"Why are you here?" asks Nicola

"Your King has sent us to you" advises Rebecca

"We have no King but Caesar" replies the Centurian

"We can take you too him, if you follow" advises Nicola

"We don't recognise you or your authority" replies the Centurian

"Him again" responds Peter

"You've met him before?" asks Mary

"Yes, in the York Dungeon" advises Nicola

"We thought we had removed him" replies John Paul

"He is obviously very stubborn" advises Nicola

"Just like a man" replies Rebecca

The Centurian and his soldiers stand firm in a ghostly mist ...

"Who are you to instruct orders" asks the Centurian

"We are here in the name of Caesar" advises John Paul

The Ghost from Christmas past now reappears …

"I know you, Centurian" says the apparition

"Yes, we have met before" replies the Centurian

"Listen to what they say to you … for yours is a fate of discontent" advises the apparition

"We have no fate … except to obey the will of Caesar" replies the Centurian

Suddenly, the sounding of a trumpet is heard in the background …

"All hail Caesar" shouts the Centurian

"Why, it's …" says Rebecca

"Yes, Gabriel" advises John Paul

The Archangel Gabriel … the messenger angel …

"Behold I bring you glad tidings … for I bring you news of great joy" advises Gabriel

"I am here to gather in the flock" advises Gabriel

"By who's authority?" asks the Roman guard

"God's authority" replies Gabriel

"We have no God but Caesar" responds the Centurian

"God has many names" advises Gabriel

"You must do as I command, or you will all be dismissed from this place for all eternity" advises Gabriel

"I am offering you all a place of sanctuary" replies Gabriel

The Centurian and Roman guard consult with their officers …

"We will do as you say" advises the Roman guard

"Our men grow weary" replies the Centurian

The Centurian issues orders to the Legion of Roman Soldiers …

"Men, put down your weapons" orders the Centurian

"We must go and leave this place, forever" advises the Centurian

"And what of me?" asks the ghost of Christmas past

"You too have found refuge and favour with God" advises Gabriel

"For all who believe in Him shall be given Eternal life" replies Gabriel

"Michael has sent me to help you John Paul" advises Gabriel

"May God bless you all and may you witness God's grace and favour" advises Gabriel

Suddenly, the mist surrounding the Roman Legion, the ghost of Christmas past and Archangel Gabriel disappear into the night ...

John Paul, Rebecca, Mary, Nicola, and Peter are left alone ...

"Did all of that really happen?" asks Peter

"Yes" advises Nicola

"It really did happen, Peter" replies Rebecca

"It wasn't a dream?" asks Peter

"No, it was all real" advises John Paul

"For nothing is impossible to God, Peter" replies Nicola

"Now, you must keep our secret" advises John Paul

All four Angels and Peter re-join the ghost walk with Mark ...

"Nice of you to join us again" says Mark

"Where have you all been?" asks Mark

"Sorry, we got side tracked by some ghostly Roman soldiers you know" advises Peter

"Yes, I know" replies Mark

"Well, we all actually popped into the pub for a swift half" advises John Paul

"Yes, sorry about that" replies Mary

"No need to apologise" responds Mark

"Now, on with the tour" advises Mark

"If only they knew" replies Peter

"If they only knew indeed Peter" advises Nicola

Nicola holds Peter's hand … he is unaware that his memory has been erased of the recent event concerning the Roman Legion …

"Now, where were we?" asks Mark

"Ghostly apparitions?" advises John Paul

"They don't really exist … do they?" asks Peter

"We will have to remain secret on that one" advises John Paul

"No one must ever know the truth" responds Nicola

ON THE LAST DAY OF CHRISTMAS

… A NEW YEAR CAME TO ME

In the finale, Rebecca, Mary, Nicola, and John Paul are invited as special guests to a New Year's Eve gala dinner in York.

The city centre it is remarkably busy with tourists flocking there to see in the New Year. Peter's infatuation with Nicola takes a twist … except things change when they all meet Steve and Sarah prior to the event.

York city centre, New Year's Eve, close to Christmas Angels shop in Low Petergate …

"Hello … fancy bumping into you again" advises Steve

"You do remember me, don't you?" asks Steve

"Of course," advises John Paul

"Sorry, we had to leave the other night, but Nicola and I were called away on an urgent personal matter" advises John Paul

"No need to explain" advises Steve

"I was wondering though, if you and all your associates would care to join us tonight, at the New Year's Eve gala dinner at the Grand Hotel?" asks Steve

It's a black-tie event" advises Steve

"You will all be our guests, naturally" advises Steve

"We would love to, we have never been to such an occasion before" advises John Paul

"Excellent, we will expect you at the Grand Hotel about 8pm" replies Steve

"It will give the ladies a chance to wear all their finery" advises Steve

"Finery?" asks Nicola

"You know all your jewels?" responds John Paul

Nicola is excited and enters Christmas Angels to tell the others the news of the exceedingly kind invitation to the New Year's Eve gala dinner at the Grand Hotel ...

The Grand Hotel is five star and has stunning views of the Minster and the cities ancient walls. The river Ouse runs along the side if it ...

John Paul re-joins Nicola in telling Rebecca and Mary the news ...

Inside Christmas Angels shop, Low Petergate ...

"We have all been invited to a New Year's Eve gala dinner by Steve and Sarah at the Noel Shop" advises John Paul

"So, they are the owners?" asks Rebecca

"Wow, it's very expensive" advises Peter

"Expensive?" asks Mary

"Yes, it must be at least £150 per head tonight" advises Peter

"Well, Steve says it's black tie and ballgowns" advises John Paul

"Oh, you will all look lovely" advises Peter

"How do we pay for such an occasion?" asks Rebecca

"We have been specially invited by Steve and Sarah and we are their guests" advises John Paul

"That's really very generous" replies Rebecca

"Yes, but where do we get such attire at short notice?" asks Nicola

"Don't worry, we will get you all sorted out" advises Peter

"It's so kind of them to invite us" advises Nicola

"What's the catch?" asks Rebecca

"There is no catch, as far as I am aware, Rebecca" advises John Paul

"Such generosity usually comes, with a condition" replies Mary

"Well, let us take it on face value and see what happens" replies John Paul

Earlier, in the centre of York, shoppers are frantically buying from various stores and Christmas Angels is also remarkably busy …

"May we purchase this Christmas scene, please?" asks a customer

"Yes, of course" replies Kate

Kate notices the difference in accent and asks a question …

"Have you come far?" asks Kate

"We're from the US of A" says a voice

"Oh, where abouts?" asks Kate

"Texas" is the response

"Are you enjoying your time in York?" asks Kate

"Oh, we absolutely love it" says a voice

"I tried to buy the York Minster … but they told me it's not for sale" says the American gentleman

Kate laughs at the response …

"The Minster?" asks Kate

"Why the Minster?" asks Kate

"Well, it would have looked so good over there" says the voice

"I've already bought London Bridge … so I thought why not?" advises the American gentleman

"London Bridge?" asks Kate

"Amazing, thank you" replies Kate

"Wonderful to meet you both" advises Kate

"You too, honey" replies the American gentleman

"Have a nice day" responds the American lady

"You too" beams Kate

Both leave Christmas Angels shop and continue to meander down the street …

"Did you hear that, Peter?" asks Kate

"What did they say?" asks Peter

"The gentleman said he was trying to buy the Minster" advises Kate

"What did you make of it?" asks Kate

"Oh, he was probably pulling your leg" advises Peter

"Did he leave his name?" asks Peter

"He said he was The President" advises Kate

"That sounds about right" advises Peter

Nicola, Mary, and Rebecca announce they have found their gowns for the event at the Grand Hotel gala dinner …

"Mine is especially with you in mind, Peter" advises Nicola

"When will I see it, Nicola?" asks Peter

"Later, before we go" advises Nicola

As early evening approaches, Nicola is ready for the gala dinner …

Peter is still on duty in Christmas angels …

"Well, how do I look, Peter?" asks Nicola

"Fabulous … like a million dollars" replies Peter

"Like a million dollars … what do you mean?" asks Nicola

"You look beautiful, Nicola" replies Peter

Nicola is dressed in a long flowing white gown decked out in crystals …

She certainly looks the part …

"Well, are we all ready" asks John Paul

"John Paul, you look very dapper in your tux" advises Peter

"Dapper" asks Nicola

"Just another word to say you look great" advises Peter

"Well, thank you kind Sir" replies John Paul

Mary and Rebecca enter the room …

They are also dressed in white ball gowns with crystals …

"Snap" advises Rebecca

"Well, you all look a picture" replies Peter

"I would say quite the finished product … for an angel" advises John Paul

"Sorry, what was that, John Paul?" asks Peter

"Oh, I am just complementing them on their gowns" replies John Paul

"Now if you can all get together, I will take your picture" asks Peter

"No, I don't think that's a good idea Peter" advises John Paul

"We must have something to record the occasion" replies Peter

"Later, Peter" asks Nicola

"OK later … what did I do hit a raw nerve or something?" asks Peter

"No, it's not like that at all Peter" advises Nicola

John Paul asks Nicola to calm Peter down …

"I have ordered you a taxi" advises Peter

"It's a pity you're not coming with us" says John Paul

"Don't worry about me I will be OK" advises Peter

"Wait up for me, Peter" replies Nicola

"I will, I promise I will" advises Peter

The Grand Hotel prides itself on delivering impeccable service and standards ...

The Concierge greets all diners on entrance ...

John Paul, Nicola, Mary, and Rebecca arrive outside the Grand Hotel ...

Steve and Sarah are inside the reception area waiting to greet all their guests ...

"Welcome" advises Steve

"You all look stunning" advises Sarah

"Angels in white" replies Steve

"How does he know?" asks Mary

"He doesn't" replies Rebecca

"It's just a compliment" advises John Paul

The Grand Hotel is a grade two listed building which stands proudly within the heart of York.

The Grand Ballroom is majestic and is expensively decorated throughout. It has tables for over 160 guests and it is tastefully decorated in the art nouveau style ...

When John Paul, Nicola, Rebecca, and Mary enter the Ballroom they are al announced ...

"May we present Christmas Angels" advises the announcer

"What's going on?" asks Mary

"Are we being announced as angels?" asks Rebecca

"No, just smile it is simply to say we are here" advises John Paul

"Well, I know I am here ... why do they need to announce it?" asks

Mary

"Just smile" advises Rebecca

Everyone is seated for dinner except for Sarah who is nowhere to be seen ...

"Have you seen Sarah?" asks Steve

"What's happened to her?" asks John Paul

Someone from another table advises that she is outside aiding some young reveller who has fallen into the river ...

"Oh my God" responds Steve

"I must go" advises Steve

"We'll accompany you" advises Rebecca

Steve, John Paul, Rebecca, Nicola, and Mary arrive on the scene and witness a young man and woman shouting for help from the river ...

"Sarah ... there you are" advises Steve

"I heard them shouting for help, so I came to investigate" replies Sarah

"I was trying to help, but I just couldn't reach them" advises Sarah

John Paul and Nicola leave the scene changing their identities and return posing as Fire and Ambulance crew ...

"That was quick" advises Steve

"We were passing" says a responder aka John Paul

"What's happened?" says a Nurse aka Nicola

Steve explains the situation and the difficulty the young couple who are in the river ...

"Where did you see them last?" asks John Paul

"Near the bridge" replies Sarah

"OK ... we'll check there, let's hope they have clung to it" advises Nicola

"Are you relatives?" asks John Paul

"No … we are just New Year's Eve party goers from the Grand Hotel"
advises Steve

"Don't worry we will get them to safety" advises John Paul

The dramatic consequences take a turn when Sarah is accidentally
pushed into the river by a drunken reveller …

"Help me" shouts Sarah

"Hold on Sarah" shouts Steve

"We've got to get them all out as soon as we can" insists John Paul

"Two flood warnings are in place as the river Ouse rises due to snow
melt it will make it even more hazardous and dangerous" advises
John Paul

"I will save her" replies Rebecca

"Me too" says Mary

Both are aided by John Paul and Nicola who are in disguise …

Chaotic scenes are now unfolding on Lendal Bridge …

After several attempts to bring the young man and woman to safety
they eventually climb back on to the riverbank, both are in distress …

"Where's my wife?" asks Steve

"What's her name?" asks Nicola

"Sarah" advises Steve

"Can you hear me, Sarah?" asks Steve

Sarah nods her head …

"OK Sarah, we are going to lay you down and you will start to feel a
warm sensation enter your body …" advises John Paul

There is no response from Sarah …

"I think she is going" advises Steve

"Quickly, we must act now" advises Nicola

A very bright light shines from Sarah's body …

"What's happening?" asks Steve

"We are healing her" advises John Paul

"Who are you?" asks Steve

"We are angels" advises John Paul

After a few minutes, things begin to change …

"She is responding" advises Nicola

Mary and Rebecca assist and look after the young man and woman …

"Are you both alright?" asks Rebecca

"What happened?" asks the young man

"Don't you remember, you were in the river?" advises Mary

"Who saved us?" asks the young woman

"We must thank them" says the young man

"We saved you … we are angels" advises Rebecca

"You are real angels?" asks the young man

"Yes … you must keep our secret and if you join hands with us now, everything will be completed" says Mary

"Completed?" asks the young woman

"What do you mean, completed?" asks the young woman

All four touch hands and a beam of light appears …

When the young man and young woman open their eyes, they are the only ones left on the riverbank …

Similarly, Steve and Sarah have witnessed the same scene unfolding …

"It's a miracle" advises Sarah

"Yet, I can't remember anything … only that I have been saved" says Sarah

"Let's go back inside the hotel" advises Steve

Back in the Grand Hotel, John Paul, Rebecca, Mary, and Nicola re-join Steve and Sarah in the ballroom ...

"What happened?" asks John Paul

"I accidently fell into the river trying to help someone in distress" says Sarah

"Real Christmas angels saved me" advises Sarah

"How do you know?" asks Rebecca

"I know inside of me ... I feel their presence" advises Sarah

"Come on Sarah, let's get you into another dress" replies Steve

"Are you sure your OK to carry on with the festivities?" asks Steve

"Yes, I am shocked, but so happy to be alive" says Sarah

"You have received a wonderful gift, Sarah ... may you be blessed with a new life this New Year" advises Mary

"May I have this dance, Nicola?" asks Peter

"You look so good in your tux ... how did you get here?" asks Rebecca

"Oh, Steve brought me here as a surprise ... and Kate too" advises Peter

"Well, have you enjoyed your time at Christmas Angels?" asks Peter

"We have just been given some wonderful news" advises Rebecca

"Our Boss has contacted us" advises John Paul

"We have been told that Christmas Angels will be our permanent base" confirms John Paul

"There is so much work to do here" replies Mary

"Our work is never done" advises Rebecca

"May Christmas Angels continue to prosper and Noel too, Steve" says John Paul

"We will all drink to that" advises Peter

HAPPY NEW YEAR

ANGEL'S EYES/CHRISTMAS ANGELS

WHITE FEATHERS APPEAR

WHEN ANGELS ARE NEAR

Copyright - Gerry Cullen
2023

PRAISE FOR AUTHOR

This book was of particular interest to me because of my line of work. The author begins by telling a little bit about himself and his life growing up. He then goes into detail about the "messages" he received prior to having open heart surgery at Leeds General Infirmary in March 2018. The author also writes about visions during his coma.
This book is a great read and it is sure to inspire and provoke discussion.
I feel this book should be taken for what it is ... one gentlemans extraordinary, unique and beautiful experience which he has chosen to share with the World.
The book, it's contents and the author himself are a true gift to the World.

*- LAURA (THE BOOKISH HERMIT) 5 STARS ***** (AMAZON)*

- BETWEEN WORLDS: MY TRUE COMA STORY

ABOUT THE AUTHOR

Gerry Cullen

 My first book, BETWEEN WORLDS: MY TRUE COMA STORY, is a true adaptation of what happened to me, before and after, having major open heart surgery at Leeds General Infirmary in March 2018.

It is a very real and true account of the "gift" I received after being in an induced coma.

My second book, SKY HIGH! COTE D'AZUR, is an adaptation of my action/adventure series of stories written for televison.

So far, I have written 8 books and over 100 Television series, to date, all out of my coma.

I had never written books or for television prior to being in a coma.

My very real and true story continues today.

TWITTER - @GerryCullen15

BOOKS BY THIS AUTHOR

Between Worlds: My True Coma Story

This true-life story includes an account of what happened to Gerry Cullen before and after waking up, having had major open heart surgery at Leeds General Infirmary in March 2018 and the "gift" from being in an induced coma.

Gerry explains his new found "gift" within the book. But where had it come from and why he received it, remains a mystery to this day.

Sky High! Cote D'azur

Nice, sunkissed jewel of the French Riviera. A popular tourist destination and playground for the rich and famous.

When a British MI6 agent goes missing after being on attachment to the Commissariat de Police in Nice, a Specialist Task Force is set up on the Cote d'Azur with Countess Suzanna Minori of Monaco under the CODE NAME: SKY HIGH!

Three "ghost" operatives are drafted in taking on various missions of danger.

Stylish, chic, gripping with just the right amount of panache!

An adrenaline rush of action ... c'est la vie!

Printed in Great Britain
by Amazon

28920873R00145